50¢

THE AMERICAN BOOK OF COMMON PRAYER

THE PRAYER BOOK WINDOW

THE BOOK OF COMMON PRAYER reads, immediately following the Preface:

The Order for Holy Communion, the Order for Morning Prayer, the Order for Evening Prayer, and the Litany, as set forth in this Book, are the regular Services appointed for Public Worship in this Church, and shall be used accordingly.

A major part of the Prayer Book Window symbolizes these three forms of service. The main portion of the left lancet symbolizes Morning and Evening Prayer, which revolve around the Bible. The right-hand lancet depicts the Holy Communion. Across the bottom of the window the Litany is indicated in the form which was habitual in the early days of the Church—a procession out-of-doors. Dominating the entire window, the central panel shows Christ as Mediator, presenting the prayers of His Church before the throne of the Almighty.

The rest of the window is devoted to history. The Prayer Book of the Church of England received its form from 1549-1662, and to represent this span we have the great figure of 1549, Archbishop Thomas Cranmer, and the corresponding figure of the 1662 revision, Bishop Cosin. But the first English Book had its roots in the past. Of this earlier period, one of the outstanding figures is Gregory the Great. He is shown to the left of Cranmer. It is also true that the development of the Prayer Book did not stop in 1662, for various self-governing Churches within the Anglican Communion have adopted revisions of their own: in Scotland, Ireland, Canada, and the United States, to name four. We therefore have a figure to typify work done on the Prayer Book in the New World, Bishop Seabury. Thus, four historical figures—Gregory, Cranmer, Cosin, and Seabury—indicate the gradual development of the Book of Common Prayer. The coats-of-arms in the window are those of archbishops and bishops who participated in the creation or development of the Book.

Woven into the very fabric of the Prayer Book, from cover to cover, is the Church Year, which affects and colors all the regular services. Therefore the small tracery areas at the top of the window are devoted to the Christian Seasons. Of these, the two dominant ones are Christmas and Easter, shown in the two largest spaces.

The American Book of Common Prayer

ITS ORIGIN AND DEVELOPMENT

BY The Very Reverend John Wallace Suter, D.D.

Dean of Washington Cathedral

and Custodian of the Standard Book of Common Prayer

AND The Reverend George Julius Cleaveland

Canon Librarian of Washington Cathedral

NEW YORK

Oxford University Press

1949

Copyright, 1949, by Oxford University Press, Inc.

Published in Commemoration of the Four Hundredth Anniversary
of the Book of Common Prayer
under the auspices of
the Cathedral Church of St. Peter and St. Paul
Washington, D. C.

Printed in the United States of America

FOREWORD

So BRIEF a survey as this monograph can only present the reader with a selection of historical findings, pointing to certain steps in the progress of the Prayer Book through the years and showing how they are related. To fill in the gaps one has to consult such works as those listed at the end of this book.

Canon Cleaveland has carefully examined the early Books and the records pertaining to them, and has written the first chapters; he has also supervised the taking of photographs and compiled the material for the Appendix. I have added a final chapter, and have performed some of the duties of an editor.

Canon Cleaveland and I are grateful to the Rev. Charles W. Lowry, Jr., Ph.D., of Chevy Chase, Maryland, for his careful perusal of the manuscript of the historical chapters and his good suggestions, though we do not hold him responsible for any opinions set forth in the book. The Cathedral authorities have been unfailingly cooperative. To Mrs. George M. Maynard we express our sincere thanks for her excellent work in preparing the manuscript.

The Prayer Book Window of Washington Cathedral, shown in the frontispiece, is the clerestory window nearest the crossing in the west wall of the north transept. It was given by Mrs. Charles Hamilton Maddox in memory

of her parents, Cora Hull Ramage and Samuel Young
Ramage. The window was made by Wilbur Herbert
Burnham in his studio in Boston.

There are four major phases of Prayer Book history.
First, everything prior to the first Book in the English
language. This includes Jewish influences, New Testament
days, the Christian Church both in the East and in the
West. Second, the period from about 1540 to 1662, the
latter date being that of the revision which is still in use in
England. Third, for the Church in the United States, the
span of years from 1789, when we achieved independence,
to the present. And fourth, the story of the translation of
the English Prayer Book, in one or another of its national
versions, into the languages of people to whom it was taken
by the missionary-minded of the several branches of Anglicanism—for instance, Prayer Books in German, French,
Swedish, Spanish, Chinese.

Of these four phases the second, that of 1540-1662 in
England, is crucial. For in that country during those years
there was fashioned a Prayer Book tradition that was to
influence deeply all future versions, in all languages.

What a period it was! Seldom have a hundred and
twenty years made so much difference to so many people.
To gain an idea of the length of that particular span, we
may recall that just one hundred and twenty years separated the inauguration of Andrew Jackson from that of
Harry S. Truman. And during the time from 1542 to 1662,
while the Prayer Book was taking shape, what else was
going on? In poetry, one thinks of Edmund Spenser, Christopher Marlowe, Shakespeare, Ben Jonson, John Donne,
George Herbert, Milton, Richard Crashaw, and John
Dryden. The prose of the King James Bible comes to mind,
as also that of Richard Hooker, Francis Bacon, Thomas
Browne, and John Bunyan. As for adventurous voyages on
land and sea, these were the days of Hakluyt, Drake,

Hawkins, Frobisher, and Raleigh. In music, there came to flower such composers as Tallis, Byrd, Orlando Gibbons; Handl, Buxtehude, and Hasler; Monteverde, Frescobaldi, di Lasso, Palestrina, and Vittoria. As for painting, it was in 1540 that Michelangelo did 'The Last Judgment,' to be followed twenty years later by his work on the dome of St. Peter's. Titian and Tintoretto were of the same period; in the Netherlands, Frans Hals and Rembrandt enriched the world of art; and the same era saw the works of Rubens, Van Dyck, Velásquez, and Murillo.

This was an age of singular vitality. People felt deeply, even tumultuously, and many of them acted violently. One need only rehearse the succession of the British crown: Henry VIII, Edward VI, Mary, Elizabeth, James I, Charles I, the Commonwealth under Cromwell, Charles II. It was an age when people expressed themselves, and gave their lives and their fortunes to exploits physical, mental, and spiritual.

From the theological and ecclesiastical thoughts and emotions of those days, from the political and social stresses and crises, from the religious convictions of people deeply committed to Christian discipleship, there emerged a pattern which shaped the public worship of thousands in succeeding generations.

John Wallace Suter

Washington

CONTENTS

		PAGE
Foreword		V
I. Colonial and Revolutionary Times		3
II. Preparation for the 1549 Book		24
III. From the 1549 to the 1662 Book		37
IV. The American Book of Common Prayer		52
V. The Prayer Book Today		69
Some Noted Prayer Books		81
Bibliography		83

ILLUSTRATIONS

The Prayer Book Window, *frontispiece*

facing page

I. The original 1549 Book of Common Prayer, title page   22

II. The 1552 Book of Common Prayer, title page   23

III. The 1559 Book of Common Prayer, title page   38

IV. The 1604 Book of Common Prayer, title page   39

V. The original 1662 Book of Common Prayer   54

VI. The 1790 Pre-standard Edition of the Book of Common Prayer, title page of the 1791 impression   55

VII. The 1892 Standard Book of Common Prayer   70

VIII. The 1928 Standard Book of Common Prayer   71

THE AMERICAN BOOK OF COMMON PRAYER

CHAPTER I

COLONIAL AND REVOLUTIONARY TIMES

J OHN CABOT put the *Matthew* out to sea in the reign of King Henry VII, and on St. John the Baptist's Day, 1497, reached the North American continent. An entry in the privy purse expenses of Henry VII reads: '1498, March 24, to Lanslot Thirlkill, of London, upon a prest for his shipp going towards the New Ilande, £20.'[1] A note found elsewhere states: 'Early in the sixteenth century a canon of St. Paul's, London, Albert de Prato, appears upon the American coast, who addressed his patron, Cardinal Wolsey, in a letter not extant, from the harbor of St. John's, Newfoundland.'[2] From such expeditions Englishmen learned of the New World.

Before the knowledge thus gained was turned to England's profit and God's glory, mighty events took place. Prior to the landing of the first settlers at James Town in 1607, England asserted her right to freedom from external ecclesiastical absolutism and made good her assertion; she fought for and won the right to be mistress in her own house. During those years the Church was reformed, its services of worship were simplified and revised, and a Book of Common Prayer was published in the vernacular. The Bible was published in English in 1539 and by royal au-

[1] William Stevens Perry, *The History of the American Episcopal Church* (Boston: J. R. Osgood & Co., 1885), vol. I, p. 2.
[2] *Ibid.*

thority ordered to be placed in every parish church that it might be read by all men. The Prayer Book, first published in 1549, revised in 1552, cast out in 1553, was revised and restored in 1559. Provoked by the danger of the Spanish Armada and made confident by victory over that mighty force, English seamen stood prepared to extend their nation's sovereignty to the New World. Naval task forces like that of Sir Francis Drake, which went forth to wipe out the sea power of England's enemies and to increase her own, and colonization expeditions like that of Sir Humphrey Gilbert, carried with them priests of the Church of England who led their fellow churchmen in the worship of Almighty God through the instrumentality of the Book of Common Prayer.

In 1553, for the first time in history, so far as is known, the Book of Common Prayer of the non-papal, reformed Catholic Church of England was taken aboard ship and carried on the high seas by men engaged in an expedition of exploration and colonization. That expedition, sent forth by Sebastian Cabot, governor 'of the mysterie and companie of the Marchants aduenturers for the discouerie of Regions, Dominions, Islands and places unknowen,' ³ was under the command of Sir Hugh Willoughby. It consisted of three ships. Master Richard Stafford, minister, accompanied the expedition as chaplain. Sebastian Cabot's order to the captain of this first fleet manned by men of the reformed Church of England was 'that the morning and evening prayer, with other common services appointed by the king's majestie, and lawes of this realme, be read and saide in every ship, daily, by the minister in the Admirall, and the marchant or some other person learned on the other ships, and the Bible or paraphrases ⁴ be read devoutly and Christianly to God's honour, and for his grace to be obtained, and had by humble and heartie praier of the Naui-

³ *Ibid.*   ⁴ Of Erasmus.

gants accordingly.' [5] Just as the men of this enterprise were destined not to reach North America but to die of exposure and hunger in the Russian Lapland, so the 1552 edition of the Book of Common Prayer, a copy of which their chaplain took with him, was destined to have a short life. In turn, however, the papal reaction which engulfed it was shortly to give way to a lasting resurrection of reformed religion.

Though the services of the 1552 Book of Common Prayer were not destined to be heard on American soil, those of the Book of 1559 were. 'Fifteen sayle of good ships,' under the command of Martin Frobisher, left Harwich May 31, 1578, and reached Frobisher Bay July 2, 1578. The fleet carried as chaplain Maister Wolfall, priest of the Church of England. He is described by Hakluyt as 'a learned man, appointed by her Majestie's Councell to be their Minister and Preacher.' [6] Of his ministrations the Rev. Richard Hakluyt,[7] rector of James Town,[8] Virginia, wrote:

> Maister Wolfall on *Winter's Fornace*, preached a godly sermon, which being ended, he celebrated also a Communion vpon the land, at the partaking whereof was the Captain of the *Anne Francis*, and many other Gentlemen, and Souldiers, Mariners, and Miners with him. The celebration of the diuine mystery was the first signe, seale, and confirmation of Christ's name, death, and passion euer knowen in these quarters. The said M. Wolfall made sermons, and celebrated the Com-

---

[5] Perry, *op. cit.*, pp. 3-4.

[6] *Ibid.*, p. 7.

[7] Richard Hakluyt's appointment as absentee rector of James Town, Virginia, proved of inestimable value to the colony in that Hakluyt in England 'screened' the clergy going to James Town to serve as chaplains, thus ensuring to the colony good men.

[8] George Maclaren Brydon, *Virginia's Mother Church* (Richmond: Virginia Historical Society, 1947), p. 1.

munion at sundry other times in seuerall and sundry ships, because the whole company could neuer meet together at any one place.[9]

To the Rev. Mr. Wolfall, priest of the reformed Church of England, belongs the signal honor of having celebrated on North American soil, so far as is known, the first service of the Holy Communion in the English tongue. To reconstruct that service, one has but to read the Order for the Administration of the Lord's Supper, or Holy Communion, as set forth in the 1559 Book of Common Prayer of the Church of England.

The year before Sir Martin Frobisher entered Frobisher's Bay, Sir Francis Drake set forth on an entirely different sort of expedition. December 10, 1577, Drake began his attempt to sail around the world. Combining adventure with profit, he plundered and destroyed Spanish ships and settlements wherever and whenever possible. On board his ship, the *Pelican*, was a priest of the Church of England, Francis Fletcher. During his journey Drake discovered Oregon and California. In a 'convenient and fit harbor' he and his men landed the first Sunday after Trinity, June 21, 1579, for repairs to his ships and for the worship of God. Drake caused a cross to be raised, declared that he took possession of the land in the name of England's queen, and affixed to the cross the arms of England. Today in Golden Gate Park, San Francisco, a great stone cross commemorates the services held on the California coast by the Rev. Francis Fletcher, chaplain of Drake's expedition, and priest of the non-papal, reformed Church of England. If the Book of Common Prayer was used on that occasion, then it was the Elizabethan Book of 1559. To the Rev. Francis Fletcher may therefore belong the honor of being the first priest to use the Book of Common Prayer of the

[9] Perry, *op. cit.*, p. 7.

Church of England on the soil of what is now the United States of America.

England was determined to colonize America and to plant on this continent an extension of her national and religious life. On June 11, 1578, Queen Elizabeth granted a patent to Sir Humphrey Gilbert 'for the inhabiting and planting of our people in America.' [10] August 4, 1583, the Tenth Sunday after Trinity, Gilbert landed at what is now St. John's, Newfoundland. Monday he took formal possession in the name of the queen. He proclaimed three laws for immediate observance. One established the Church of England as the Church of the colony, declaring that 'in [its] publique exercise [religion] should be according to the Church of England.' [11] The loss of one of his ships caused Gilbert to abandon the attempt at colonization and return to England. He perished on the return trip, being last seen at the stern of his sinking ship, with a book in his hand, and probably the Book of Common Prayer, saying, 'We are as neare to heaven by sea as by land.' [12]

Sir Walter Raleigh obtained from Queen Elizabeth a new patent giving him and his heirs the rights and privileges hitherto granted Sir Humphrey Gilbert. These new letters patent required that the government of the colony be established according to the law of England and that its religion be that of the established Church. Acting under the patent, Raleigh sent out two ships under Phillip Amadas and Arthur Barlowe. The ships reached the coast of North Carolina July 4, 1584. After spending several weeks in coastal exploration, Amadas and Barlowe enticed or forced two natives, Manteo and Wanchese, to accompany the expedition back to England. The years these two Indians spent in England made a profound impression on them. Manteo became the friend of the English for life and

[10] *Ibid.*, p. 8.
[11] *Ibid.*
[12] *Ibid.*

Wanchese an undying foe. Elizabeth called the new land Virginia and gave Raleigh a monopoly of all trade with the colony. He made plans for greater colonization. It is estimated that in all he spent over a million dollars in attempting to colonize the New World.

A second expedition was sent out under the command of Sir Richard Grenville, a relative of Raleigh. This fleet of seven ships left Plymouth on Good Friday, April 9, 1585, to colonize New Virginia. The colony, one hundred and eight men under the governorship of Ralph Lane, was established August 17, 1585, on the north end of Roanoke Island. The Rev. Thomas Hariot, priest of the reformed Church of England, was its historian. To this priest and inventor of algebraic notation, we are indebted for our first knowledge of the edibility of the potato and the use of tobacco. John White, artist of the colony, drew sketches of wild and human life, which are extant.[13] Hariot wrote in *A Briefe and True Report of the New Found Land of Virginia:*

> Many times and in euery towne where I came, according as I was able, I made declaration of the contents of the Bible, that therein was set foorth the true and onely God, and his mightie workes, that therein was conteined the true doctrine of saluation through Christ, with many particularities of Miracles and chiefe points of Religion as I was able then to vtter, and thought fit for the time. And although I told them the booke materially and of itselfe was not of any such virtue, as I thought they did conceiue, but onely the doctrine therein conteined; yet would many be glad to touch it, to embrace it, to kisse it, to hold it to their breastes and heads, and stroke ouer all their body with it, to show their hungry desire of that knowledge which was spoken of.[14]

---

[13] In the British Museum.   [14] Perry, *op. cit.*, p. 12.

During the life of the colony, Indians and colonists joined in receiving from Dr. Hariot instruction out of the Holy Bible, and in worship according to the 1559 Book of Common Prayer. Governor Lane's mismanagement of the colony and the mistreatment of the Indians brought about a situation which prompted the colonists to accept Drake's offer of June 8, 1586, to return to England. Two weeks after their departure from Roanoke Island, three ships under the command of Sir Richard Grenville arrived bringing supplies. Grenville, finding the settlement deserted, left fifteen men with two years' supply of provisions to hold the fort while he returned to England.

A new group of colonists under the governorship of John White, this group numbering one hundred fifty, some of whom were women, arrived at Roanoke Island June 22, 1587. Raleigh gave the colony 100 pounds sterling, the income of which was to be used for 'planting the Christian religion, and advancing the same.' [15] The colonists repaired the fort and the houses deserted by the earlier group and planted gardens. August 13, 1587, the Indian Manteo, who had returned from England, was baptized. The sacramental act was administered on the Ninth Sunday after Trinity, and the service used was that of the 1559 Book of Common Prayer. To the Rev. Thomas Hariot belongs the honor of being the first clergyman of the Church of England to administer on American soil the sacrament of Holy Baptism according to the Book of Common Prayer. The next Sunday, Virginia, the daughter of Ananias and Eleanor Dare, was baptized. She was born August 18, 1587, and was the first white child baptized on American soil. Governor White returned to England for more colonists and supplies, leaving his daughter, Eleanor, and grandchild, Virginia Dare. He expected to return speedily. Having arrived in England, he found his ships and men were re-

[15] *Ibid.*, p. 18.

quired for the defence of England against the Spanish Armada. After the Armada was defeated he endeavored to return but was forced to turn back. Eventually, in 1591, he did get back to Roanoke Island. On his arrival he found the colony gone, the site abandoned, and the letters C R O carved on a tree; on a palisade entrance was the word C R O A T O A N. It had been agreed that if the colony were to move, the place to which it went was to be named —with a cross carved above it if the colonists were in distress, and with no cross if there had been no violence. No cross was found, nor were the colonists ever traced. Thus ended the first real attempt at colonization on the part of England and the Church of England.

Neither the nation nor the Church abandoned the effort to plant the English way of life and religion upon these shores. On Easter Day, March 31, 1605, and 'in the name of God,' an expedition under the command of George Waymouth sailed from Dartmouth Haven. Rosier, the recorder of this enterprise, says the promoters were motivated by the desire for 'not a little present profit, but a public good, and the true zeal of promulgating God's holy Church, by planting Christianity.' [16] They landed on Monhegan Island off the coast of Maine on Whitsunday and, to quote Rosier, 'all with great joy praised God for his unspeakable goodness, who had from so apparent danger delivered us, and directed us upon this day into so secure an harbor, in remembrance whereof we named it Pentecost Harbor.' [17] The day following, Monday, May 20, 1605, Waymouth and thirteen men, after prayers, departed in the shallop and went up the river Kennebec on a tour of inspection. Having traveled forty miles, they returned, captured five Indians, and Sunday, June 16, 1605, began the voyage back to England. The Book of Common Prayer used at the erection of the cross, marking the discovery and claim to

[16] *Ibid.*, p. 27.   [17] *Ibid.*

the land, must have been that of James I (1604), from which the state prayers were read. This book differed little from that of 1559. Waymouth's expedition paved the way for a serious attempt to colonize North America.

April 10, 1606, Sir Ferdinando Gorges and Sir John Popham, both churchmen, obtained a royal charter authorizing them to colonize a strip of land as wide as from upper Nova Scotia to lower South Carolina. June 1, 1607, they sent forth two ships, the *Mary and John* and the *Gift of God*. These ships, with one hundred souls aboard, arrived at Monhegan Island in August, 1607. A manuscript in the Lambeth Library, 'A Relation of a Voyage to Sagadahoc,' tells of the landing of this colony:

> Sunday being the 9th of August [1607], in the morning the most part of our whole company of both our ships landed on this island, the which we call St. George's Island, where the cross standeth, and there we heard a sermon delivered unto us by our preacher, giving God thanks for our happy meeting and safe arrival [the ships had been separated at sea] into the country, and so returned aboard again.[18]

It was the Tenth Sunday after Trinity. The chaplain was the Rev. Richard Seymour. His is the first sermon known to have been delivered in what is now New England. August 19, 1607, a site was chosen for the settlement. A fort was built, a church erected, and homes were constructed for the colonists. Services according to the 1604 Book of Common Prayer were held as required by Christian duty and civil law. Things did not go well with the colony. Having lost a ship, they built another, the *Virginia*, the first ship built in America. Because of the harshness of the weather, the attitude of the savages, and the death of their

[18] *Ibid.*, p. 32.

leader, they returned home, some sailing to England in the first American-made vessel.

In 1606, James I granted a charter establishing the Virginia Company, giving the members authority to colonize Virginia. Three ships, the *Susan Constant*, the *Goodspeed*, and the *Discovery*, under command of Captain Christopher Newport, left Blackwell, England, on December 19, 1606, for Virginia. Aboard one ship was the missionary priest, the Rev. Robert Hunt, formerly vicar of the parish of Reculver, England. As the Rev. George Maclaren Brydon, D.D., has shown, the Rev. Richard Hakluyt, D.D., one of the incorporators of the London Company, had accepted the position of rector of James Town, Virginia, and sent Hunt to be his vicar.[19] The Rev. Robert Hunt was the right man for a difficult task. Captain John Smith wrote concerning him that he was 'an honest, religious, and courageous Divine; during whose life our factions were oft qualified, our wants and greatest extremities so comforted, that they seemed easie in comparison of what we endured after his memorable death.' [20]

On the Third Sunday after Easter the colonists entered Chesapeake Bay. After weeks of exploration they chose the (then called) peninsula of James Town, named earlier in honor of James I, as the site of their first town. May 13, 1607, the day of the choice of a site, they opened their sealed orders and set up their government with Edward-Maria Wingfield as president of the council. Whitsunday, May 24, 1607, the colonists, who with Captain Newport had ascended the James river as far as the falls below Richmond, spent the day feasting, having as their guest King Powhatan. As night approached they erected a cross just below the falls, proclaimed James I king of the territory, and prayed for him and their own prosperity. The prayer used for the king was in all probability the state prayer for

[19] *Ibid.*, p. 31   [20] *Ibid.*, p. 42.

the monarch which, appropriately revised, now appears in
our American Book of Common Prayer as the first prayer
for the President of the United States of America.
Captain John Smith, savior of the colony, in *Advertise-
ments for the Unexperienced Planters of New England*, a
book dedicated to George Abbot, Archbishop of Canterbury, thus describes the religious life of the first successful
colony on American soil:

> When I first went to Virginia, I well remember, wee
> did hang an awning (which is an old saile) to three or
> four trees to shadow us from the Sunne, our walls were
> rales of wood, our seats unhewed trees, till we cut
> plankes; our Pulpit a bar of wood nailed to two neigh-
> boring trees; in foule weather we shifted into an old
> rotten tent, for wee had few better, and this came by the
> way of adventure for new. This was our Church, till
> wee built a homely thing like a barne, set upon cratchets,
> covered with rafts, sedge, and earth; so was also the
> walls; the best of our houses of the like curiosity, but
> the most parte farre much worse workmanship, that
> could neither well defend wind nor raine, yet wee had
> daily Common Prayer morning and evening, every Sun-
> day two Sermons, and every three moneths the holy
> Communion, till our Minister died. But our Prayers
> daily, with an Homily on Sundaies, we continued two
> or three yeares after, till more Preachers came.[21]

They did come, those preachers, and they did good
work. But let it be remembered to the credit of those
colonists, rough, able men, that without a minister, without or separated from wives and children, alone in a wilder-
ness, they were unashamed to worship God through the
use of the Book of Common Prayer: without clergy they

[21] *Ibid.*, pp. 45-46.

were faithful in its use and in reading and re-reading the Homilies [22] of the Church. In other instances men came to America to establish a form of worship other than that of the Church of their fathers, but these men came to extend the government and culture of England and to establish her Church on American soil. This Church had had as its manual of worship and chief focus of unity, from 1549 on, the Book of Common Prayer.

There had been misunderstanding among these first settlers, and bitter jealousy arose. The Rev. Robert Hunt labored to settle their disputes and to establish peace among them. He succeeded, and on June 21, 1607, gathered the James Town colonists before God's Board for divine worship, preached to them, and celebrated with them the Holy Communion. We cannot recover the words of his memorable sermon but we can recover the words of the service, the Collect for the Day, and the Holy Scripture; for June 21, 1607, was the Third Sunday after Trinity, and the Holy Scripture appointed for the Epistle (in the 1604 Book of Common Prayer) was 1 Peter v. 5-11. The Epistle was written in the language of the Great Bible of 1539. The passage, however, has remained, with slight changes—from the 1549 Book of the Church of England to the present Book of Common Prayer used in the Protestant Episcopal Church of the United States, the direct descendant of the James Town church:

SUBMIT your selues euery man one to another, knyt your selues together in lowlynes of minde. For God resisteth the proud, and geueth grace to the humble. Submit your selues therfore under the mightie hād of God, that he may exalt you when the tyme is come. Cast all your care upon him: for he careth for you. Be sober,

[22] By reading the Book of Homilies set forth in the time of Elizabeth we can read the words they heard as they gathered for worship.

and watche: for your aduersary the deuil as a roaryng
Lyon, walketh about, sekyng whom he may deuour:
whom resist stedfast in the fayth, knowyng that the
same affliccions are appointed unto your brethren that
are in the worlde. But the God of all grace whiche hath
called us unto his eternall glorye by Christ Jesu, shall
his owne selfe (after ye haue suffered a lytle affliccion)
make you perfect, settle, strength, and stablishe you. To
hym be glory and dominion for euer and euer.

And the Gospel appointed for the day, taken from Luke
15, ended with these pertinent words: 'Lykewise I saye
unto you, shall there be joy in the presence of the Angels
of god, ouer one synner that repenteth.' The colonial
jealousy stopped and the quarreling ended where all discord should cease, at the Table of the Lord.

Five weeks later the colonists, with their priest, gathered
again at the Table of the Lord to partake of the Blessed
Sacrament and pray for the safety of Captain Newport and
those with him who were going back to England. They
would report and return later with more colonists and supplies. Unlike previous efforts at colonization, the James
Town venture had proved successful.

Historical sources list these significant James Town
events:

John Laydon and Anne Burras in 1608 were united in
the bonds of holy matrimony by the Rev. Robert Hunt,
vicar of James Town. The Indian maiden, Pocahontas, was
instructed in the Christian religion, baptized by the Rev.
Alexander Whitaker, minister at Henricus, Virginia, and
given the Christian name, Rebecca. The Rev. Richard
Buck, Hunt's successor at James Town, performed the
marriage service which united Rebecca Pocahontas and
John Rolfe. The Rev. Mr. Buck was the chaplain of the
first legislative assembly ever to meet on American soil.

It assembled in the church at James Town, August, 1619, and the sentences read by Mr. Buck were without doubt the state prayers of the Church of England, together with other devotions from the Book of 1604.

The Virginia Company was established not by men who desired to escape from the Church of England but by men who believed in it and were loyal to it. The missionary spirit was neither dead nor dormant in the colonial era; on the contrary there were many Christian hearts back of this enterprise.

The gallant Earl of Southampton, the Ferrars, Haklyut, and Sandys were members of the Virginia Company of London, under whose auspices the Colony of Virginia was founded and nursed in its infancy. In their view, the chief end of the enterprise was the 'plantation of the Church in the New World,' wholly given to idolatry, and the diffusion of the light of the Gospel among the Indians, who had so long sat in darkness and in the shadow of death. It was their influence which procured the insertion in charters and like documents of those 'saving clauses' which redeemed the movement from utter worldliness. These persons took care that sermons should be preached frequently before the Virginia Company, to keep before their minds the truth that the chief end of the enterprise was to plant the banner of the cross in the camp of Satan. In 1609 Crashaw, the father of the poet, preached before the Company a rousing missionary sermon, the first ever preached by a priest of the Church of England to those about to carry her name to the New World. To Lord Delaware, the captain-general, who was present, and about to sail for Virginia, he said in conclusion: 'Thy ancestor took a king prisoner on the field of battle with his own hands; but thou shalt take the Devil captive in his own kingdom, and thus the honor of thy house shall be greater at the last than at the first. You are a general of Englishmen, you go to commend Christianity to the heathen: then practise it yourself.' [23]

The Very Reverend John Donne, who wrote the *Pseudo-Martyr* urging English Jesuit priests to return to the Church of England and become loyal English churchmen, preached before the Company:

> You have your charters, seals, and commissions; what you lack is the Holy Ghost. This seals the Great Seal, and authenticates authority. Without it your patents and commissions will be but feeble crutches; with the breath of the Holy Spirit they will be wings on which you will fly the faster. Those of you who are young may live to see that you have made this island, which is the suburb of the Old World, a bridge, a galley, to the New, to join all to that world which shall never grow old—the kingdom of heaven.[24]

In a spirit of patriotism, loyal churchmanship, and Christian zeal, the men of the Virginia Company of London planned, executed, and nourished the colonization of Virginia. They were men who loved and used, as we love and use, the Book of Common Prayer. Their Prayer Book, that of 1604, was a book revised thrice. Ours is the same book seven times revised, the latest revision being that of 1928.

In 1619, a year before the Pilgrims landed, a Dutch ship arrived at James Town with twenty negro slaves. For the first time in history the white man, the black, and the red met on the American continent. The enslavement of black men in England and America was wrong—as wrong as the

---

[23] 'Addresses and Historical Papers before the Centennial Council of the Diocese of Virginia, 1785-1885,' published by the Theological Seminary, Diocese of Virginia (New York: Thomas Whittaker, 1885), p. 31.
[24] *Ibid.*, p. 32.

enslavement of white men in Africa. It is not generally known that Bishop John Cosin, author of many of the 1662 prayers in our Prayer Book, gave five hundred pounds for the liberation of white men from African slavery, or that Bishop Sanderson of Lincoln and Richard Baxter both raised their voices against the slave trade. The Rev. Morgan Godwyn, clergyman of the Church of England in Virginia, was, according to the Rev. Philip Slaughter, D.D., the first to attack the practice of slavery in America. The Society for the Propagation of the Gospel in Foreign Parts was organized in 1700 as an agency through which English churchmen might minister to the souls of the white, black and red men in Virginia. That society poured priests, Bibles, and Prayer Books into those colonies which were destined, in the providence of God, to become the United States of America. And to that venerable society the Colonial Church to a great degree owed its very being. The Church planted in Virginia at James Town continued and, liberated from English ecclesiastical control at the time of the American Revolution, was reorganized under the name of the Protestant Episcopal Church in Virginia. It retained the Book of Common Prayer in all essentials as it was before the Revolution, save for the deletion of the name of the king and the state prayers, and the substitution of prayers for the American authorities and the Congress of the United States of America.

By the beginning of the Revolutionary War, not only in the colony of Virginia but also in the other colonies, the Church of England was functioning, and in several cases was established by law as the state church. Maryland became a royal colony in 1688, and by the transformation from proprietary to royal government the Church of England became the Maryland state church and the 1662 Book of Common Prayer the official book of worship. There were forty-four priests in Maryland, at the start of the war, leading their people in devotion and life according to the directives of the Book of Common Prayer.

Massachusetts, settled by Separatists (Pilgrims) September 6, 1620, had churchmen within her borders as early as 1622. Thomas Morton, living at Merrymount in 1622, suffered at the hands of the non-conformists because of his loyal attachment to his Church. As early as 1633, churchmen of the Massachusetts Bay colony, in the face of marked opposition, worshipped God in accordance with the provisions of the Book of Common Prayer. In 1686 James II made Massachusetts a royal colony, by which act he established, as in Maryland, the Church of England as the state church and the Book of Common Prayer of 1662 as the official manual of public worship. The non-conformists, thinking that the English Revolution which placed William and Mary on the throne would result in the disestablishment of the Church, cast the royal governor into prison and expelled the clergy. To their chagrin, William did not disestablish the Church of England but reaffirmed its official status, whereupon the governor was released and the clergy permitted to return. Under the leadership of the Rev. N. E. Keith, a representative of the Society for the Propagation of the Gospel, a period of church building and expansion took place, and by the time political separation from England arrived the Church in Massachusetts was well developed.

Connecticut, settled by Separatists and non-conformists, was during its early years antagonistic to the Church of England. Indeed, the feeling against the Church and her clergy was so pronounced it was not until after the opening of the eighteenth century that Prayer Book services were tolerated in the area. In 1708 churchmen were taxed for the support of Congregational ministers. The Society for the Propagation of the Gospel sent missionary clergy into Connecticut, and the cause of the Church of England was further strengthened by the unexpected conversion and entrance into the priesthood of several Yale College faculty members. It has been estimated that during the ten following years one out of every ten Yale graduates entered the Church of England. At the opening of the struggle for American independence there were sixteen clergymen and twenty-five organized parishes in Connecticut.

New York, discovered by an English churchman in Dutch employ, and colonized by the Dutch, was brought under English control in 1664 by an expedition led by the Duke of York. Following a revolt against English rule, it was reconquered by the English in 1674, and the Dutch governor, Stuyvesant, surrendered the colony with the stipulation that the Dutch should enjoy liberty of conscience and worship. In 1665 New York became a royal colony and the Church of England, with its Book of Common Prayer of 1662, was established by law. Following establishment, church development went forward rapidly, church buildings arose, and congregations increased. When the Revolution was over and the young nation established, the Church in New York was strong enough to ask for and support its own bishop.

Pennsylvania, founded by the Friends, was established under a charter which stipulated that, whenever a sufficient number of planters desired, the services of a Church of England clergyman should be granted them. A request for a clergyman was made in 1694 and refused by the Pennsylvania authorities. Litigation followed, and the Friends were required by law to grant the request of the Pennsylvania churchmen. The next year a church was built in Pennsylvania and Prayer Book services were held. Christ Church, Philadelphia, was built in 1700; it was rebuilt in the years 1727-1744. In this church was held the 1789 General Convention of the Protestant Episcopal Church. The Rev. William White, assistant rector before

the Revolution, was elected chaplain to the Continental
Congress in 1775. He became rector of Christ Church in
1777. On July 6, 1776, in the rectory of the Rev. Mr.
Duché, then rector of Christ Church, it was resolved to
eliminate from the services of the Book of Common Prayer
the intercessions for the king of England.

Early in colonial history churchmen lived in New
Hampshire, New Jersey, and Delaware, and contended
against odds for the right to worship God according to
the Book of Common Prayer after the manner of their
fathers. At the close of the Revolution the Church in
these states was numerically weak. Georgia, also, was weak
in so far as the Church was concerned. Colonization in
Georgia began in 1733. Contributions gathered throughout England, by direction of the Archbishop of Canterbury, assisted the colonizing. The Rev. John Wesley and
his brother Charles went there as missionaries. Their
father, the Rev. Samuel Wesley, contributed a chalice and
paten for the celebration of the Holy Communion. In 1758
the Church of England was established as the state church.

North and South Carolina originally constituted one
colony whose charter established the Church of England
there. The first church in what is now South Carolina was
built in Charles Town in 1681; the first church in what is
now North Carolina seems to have been built in Edenton
in 1703. The Society for the Propagation of the Gospel
worked vigorously in the Carolinas, and many men went
from England to serve there. Toleration seems to have been
enjoyed by dissenters. About one hundred Church of
England clergymen went to South Carolina as a result of
the establishment. At the time of the Revolution public
worship according to the way of the Church of England,
as set forth in the Book of Common Prayer, was offered
in every colony to the one God and Father of all mankind.

In 1776 the priests and people who belonged to the Church of England, by law established, were politically divided. During the Revolution some left the country rather than rebel against the king, while others cast their lot with the struggle for American freedom. Many a Prayer Book of 1776 or earlier has lines drawn through the state prayers and hand-written alterations to make it serve churchmen committed to the American cause. The clergy who opposed the Revolution either left the country or were driven out. Those patriots, citizens or clergymen, who believed that the colonies under God ought to be free and independent, poured into the struggle for liberty their substance and their lives. Among them were Richard Henry Lee, who moved the adoption of the Declaration of Independence; Thomas Jefferson, vestryman of St. Anne's Parish, who with others wrote the Declaration; Patrick Henry, who aroused in his fellow citizens a spirit of rebellion against tyranny; George Washington, who abandoned his own affairs to lead his fellow countrymen in the battle for liberty and preside over the government of the new nation in the early years; Robert Morris, who placed his personal fortune at the disposal of his country; Benjamin Franklin, vestryman of Christ Church, Philadelphia, co-founder of Philadelphia Academy (later the University of Pennsylvania) and co-author of the Declaration of Independence. All were members of the Church of England and products of her devotional life, having been brought up to know and worship and serve God with the help of the Book of Common Prayer. Three-fourths of the signers of the Declaration of Independence were members of the Church of England in the colonies—a Church soon to be liberated from the ecclesiastical control of the Bishop of London and the English Parliament and to be renamed the Protestant Episcopal Church in the United States of America.

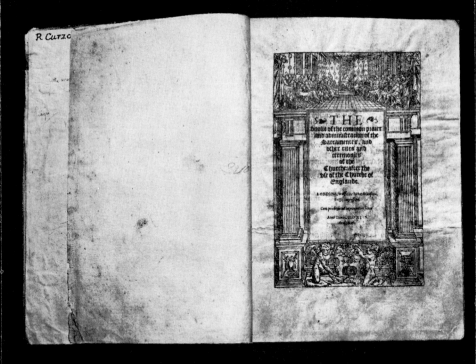

Photo by T. Horydczak, Washington

THE ORIGINAL 1549 BOOK OF COMMON PRAYER, TITLE PAGE. The book is owned by Washington Cathedral Library. This page notes it is the work of Richard Grafton and was printed in March, 1549. The colophon reads, 'Imprinted at London in Fletestrete, at the signe of the Sunne over against the Conduyte by Edvvarde VVhitechurche. The .xvi.daye of Iune, the yeare of our Lorde, 1549.' The volume therefore is a combined production of the two royal printers, Richard Grafton and Edward Whitchurche. *S. T. C. 16272* is written on the first page of the book, and *R. Curzon, Parham* on the upper left-hand corner of the front cover. The book is complete and in good condition except for minor repairs to a few pages. It shows evidence of having been rebound. The pages measure 7¾ by 11 inches but apparently have been trimmed. The 1549 Book of Common Prayer was prepared by a committee headed by Archbishop Cranmer. Thirlby, in the time of Queen Mary a 'degrader' of Cranmer, was one of the compilers. An act of Parliament ordered the Book in use on Whitsunday, June 9th, 1549. The Anglican Communion celebrated the four hundredth anniversary of this volume on June 5, Whitsunday, in 1949.

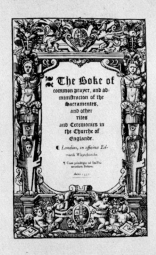

Photo by T. Horydczak, Washington

THE 1552 BOOK OF COMMON PRAYER, TITLE PAGE—a Pickering reprint of an edition originally printed by Edward Whitchurche. The pages measure 9 by 14 inches. This Second Book of Edward VI is a revision of the 1549 Book and was made under the influence of Martin Bucer, Peter Martyr, and à Lasco. It is a Protestant alteration of the more Catholic Book of 1549, but it failed to satisfy the continental reformers. It contains several splendid features which are in the American Book of Common Prayer, such as the preparatory sections of Morning and Evening Prayer, which consist of the Scripture Sentences, the Exhortation, the General Confession and Absolution. Another of its contributions to later editions is the Ten Commandments and the responses in the Order for the Administration of the Holy Communion. The Book contains the 'Black Rubric' which asserts that kneeling during the reception of the Holy Communion does not constitute eucharistic adoration. It was ordered in use on All Saints' Day, November 1, 1552. During the Catholic reaction under Queen Mary it was used until a sufficient number of Latin breviaries and missals could be obtained. The volume illustrated here is in the Washington Cathedral Library.

Just as these men and their neighbors felt the colonies needed separation from England, a new government, a closer federal union, revised laws, and a new national name, so the colonial members of the Church of England believed their Church needed, in addition to ecclesiastical separation from the Mother Church, an internal spiritual unity, a more democratic constitution, a Prayer Book of its own, and a new ecclesiastical name. There was not too much disagreement as to the name, for almost immediately we find churchmen calling themselves and one another members of the Protestant Episcopal Church. However, there was disagreement as to what the Prayer Book should contain. Some, like Benjamin Franklin, who influenced the thought of William White, wanted a drastic revision of the 1662 Book. Others, the members of King's Chapel, Boston, desired a Prayer Book which was Unitarian in theology. Others, especially in Connecticut, wanted a Book containing a liturgy for the Lord's Supper which would agree with that of the Scottish Church. The churchmen of Virginia wanted to retain the theology, devotion, and discipline of the 1662 Book of the Mother Church as little changed as was compatible with the new political and ecclesiastical situation. Yet others wished a Book of Common Prayer in which Calvinistic theology and Presbyterian polity should be dominant. In the providence of God, wise judgment prevailed and the Protestant Episcopal Church, formed of the liberated colonial churches, adopted, at the 1789 General Convention, a Book of Common Prayer, ordered in use on and after October 1, 1790, which was an American revised version of the English Book of Common Prayer. As such, it was the lineal descendant of the 1549 Book used first on Whitsunday, June 9, 1549— the four hundredth anniversary of which the Churches of the entire Anglican Communion throughout the world celebrated on Whitsunday, June 5, 1949.

CHAPTER II

PREPARATION FOR THE 1549 BOOK

D R. GEORGE HODGES, former dean of Episcopal Theological School, Cambridge, Massachusetts, wrote, in 1899: 'In the Prayer Book, part goes back to the days when the worship of the Church was in the Hebrew tongue; for example, the Psalms, and the Hebrew word *Amen*. Part belongs to the age when the great number of Christians spoke Greek, when even the Church of Rome was a Greek mission; the general structure of the Communion Office is of this period, and the Prayer of St. Chrysostom is a familiar reminder of it.' He continued:

> Part was made in the centuries when the common language of Christian people was Latin; whereof the very words remain in the titles of the Venite, the Te Deum, and other Canticles. Finally, as the Greeks had translated the Hebrew into Greek, and the Latins had translated the Greek into Latin, the English translated the Latin into English. Each made changes by addition and subtraction, as changes were made in cathedrals, as houses are altered by each generation of occupants. But the identity of the book, like the identity of the building, continued.[1]

The 1549 Book of Common Prayer, therefore, was the product of a creative and transforming past. Three great

[1] 'The Churchman,' New York, April 22, 1899.

Christian humanists, the trio of Oxford reformers, Dean John Colet, Desiderius Erasmus, and Sir Thomas More, were instrumental in opening the eyes of English churchmen to the way of truer and richer worship. Influenced by the learning of Pico Della Mirandola, Italian humanist, Catholic count, and papal ambassador to the Diet of Speyer, John Colet based his preaching upon the Word of God and inspired others to look there for a knowledge of salvation and understanding of the character of that morality which is set forth in the Old and New Testaments as righteousness of life. By his Greek New Testament with a Latin translation, his *Handbook of the Christian Knight*, his ridicule of faked miracles, his oft-expressed scorn of unscholarly Scholasticism, and his *Paraphrases of the New Testament*, Desiderius Erasmus prodded the minds of men out of superstition and ignorance and aroused in many a love for intellectual honesty and liturgical integrity. Sir Thomas More, both in his *Utopia* and in his conduct, evoked a concern for a joyous religion—one which expressed itself in interest in others as well as in individual spiritual development before God. These men and others like them made a profound impression upon the thinking of their time. Their age was characterized by an awakened interest in learning. Men began to question existing customs and institutions, to become aware of the need for, and the means of, improvement, and to strive for enrichment of life. Such ages are glorious but dangerous, for in them men may lose heart and become reactionary, plunge rashly into ungoverned excess and become destructive, or, while holding fast to what is good, move onward to that which is better. The latter, in the main, was most evident in the liturgical development which came to flower in the 1549 Book of Common Prayer.

The desire to hold fast to that which is good while moving forward to something better motivated both a

Cardinal in Spain and an Archbishop in Germany. In Spain, Cardinal Quignon, in response to a papal directive of Clement VII, produced a reformed breviary, which, in 1535 after Clement's death, was published with the approval of Paul III. The *Breviarum Romanum Nuper Reformatum* met with instant opposition, but before it was prohibited it passed through one hundred editions. Archbishop Cranmer obtained one of the earlier editions of this work, mastered its content, and used it in the formation of the Book of Common Prayer. In Germany, the Prince Elector and Archbishop of Cologne, Hermann von Wied, responding to the influence of the Lutheran Reformation, employed Bucer, Melanchthon, and Sarcerius to prepare a revision of the services used in his jurisdiction. The result was a sane work of liturgical reformation, published in German in 1543 and translated into English in 1547 under the title, *A Simple and Religious Consultation of Us, Hermann by the Grace of God Archbishop of Cologne.* For his liturgical audacity, Archbishop Hermann was rewarded with excommunication. This book, like Quignon's, exerted a strong influence on Archbishop Cranmer and his associate reformers, and portions of each may to this day be found in the Book of Common Prayer.

Long before the liturgical reformation, many Englishmen were dissatisfied with the complex nature of the offices. In 1516 the Sarum Breviary was reformed; in the years 1530-1533 the Psalter was published in both Latin and English, the Sarum Breviary was again revised and purged of papalism, and the First Primer of Henry VIII was issued in the language of the people.

The 1545 Primer was not a new invention but rather a revision of a book long popular in England. The 1533 Primer, republished in 1539 and in 1545 under Henry VIII, was also published during the reigns of Edward VI and Elizabeth. It did more than anything else to condition the hearts and minds of Englishmen to an appreciation and use of the vernacular offices and communion service as set forth later, in the time of Edward VI, in the Book of Common Prayer. The Primer, issued by authority of Henry VIII and printed by Richard Grafton, was the basis of the primers of Edward and Elizabeth. Henry's 1545 Primer was by his direction printed in both Latin and English, and contained

> The Kalendre, The kynges highnes iniuction, The praier of oure Lorde, The salutation of the angel, The Crede or article[s] of the faith, The ten commaundementes, Certein graces, The Matyns, The Euensong, The Complin, The Seuen psalmes, The Letany, The Dirige, The Commendations, The Psalmes of the passion, The passion of the Lorde, and Certein godly praiers, for sundry purposes.[2]

The wide-spread use of these primers throughout England proved an effective preparation for the Book of Common Prayer, and their continued use after the Book of Common Prayer was set forth, and even up to the reign of Elizabeth, shows the hold they had upon the human heart.

Under the leadership of William Warham, Archbishop of Canterbury, the members of the Convocations of Canterbury and York were led in 1532 to accept Henry VIII as Supreme Head in earth of the Church of England *so far as the law of Christ allows;* and in 1534 by Act of Parliament Henry was declared Supreme Head in earth of the Church of England—without the saving clause added by the clergy. The breach with Rome had taken place, and the two Convocations, apart from Rome, were now joined under one central authority. Liturgical reformation could begin.

[2] William Keatinge Clay, editor for the Parker Society, *Private Prayers of the Reign of Queen Elizabeth* (London: Cambridge University Press, 1851), p. 3.

Dissatisfied with previous attempts to give the people of England an English translation of the Holy Scriptures, Thomas Cromwell persuaded Miles Coverdale to undertake a new translation in order to bring forth a more thoughtful revision of the Matthew Bible, which itself had been to a great extent Coverdale's work. Bishop Coverdale went to Paris with Richard Grafton to publish there the newly translated Bible. Learning of the project, the Inquisition attempted to destroy the sheets and prevent the publication, but Grafton and Coverdale managed to foil the plot, save the sheets, and move the presses to England. There the Great Bible was issued in 1539. It was called the Great Bible because it was lectern size. From this Bible have come the Comfortable Words in our communion service and the Psalter in our Prayer Book. Aware of the economic loss which could result from outside interference with printing, Henry VIII gave to Grafton and Whitchurche a commission as King's Printers with the sole right to print liturgical books. The royal privilege read:

> Where in tyme past it hath been usually accustomed; that theis bookes of divine service, that is to say, the masse-book, the antyphoner, the himptuall, the porteaus and the prymer, both in Latyn and Englyshe of Sarum use, for the province of Canterbury, have been printed by Strangiers in other and strange countreys, partly to the great losse and hindrance of our subjectes, who both have the sufficient arte, feate, and treade of Printing, and by imprinting such bookes myght profitably and to thuse of the commonwelthe be set on worke, and partly to the setting forthe of the bysshop of Rome's usurped authoritie . . . We of our Grace especiall have granted and given privilege to our wel-biloved subjects, Richard Grafton and Edward Whitchurch, citizens of London,

that they and their assignes, and noon other persons . . .
have liberty to prynte the bookes abovesaid.[3]

Some of the bishops opposed the authorization and dis-
tribution of the Great Bible. These objectors were brought
before Henry VIII, who asked if to their knowledge there
were any heresies in the new translation. 'We are unable to
detect any,' they replied; whereupon the King said, 'In
God's name let it go forth among the people.' Forth it
went, and continued through the King James, the English
Revised, the American Revised, and the Revised Standard
versions—all revisions of the Great Bible—to win an in-
creasing entrance into the hearts of English-speaking
people. Without the authorization of the Great Bible, or
some other similar English Bible, the 1549 Book of Common Prayer would have been a liturgical impossibility.

At the top of the frontispiece of the Great Bible, God is
represented from within a cloud saying, 'The word which
goeth forth from me shall not return to me empty, but
shall accomplish whatsoever I will have done.' To the
prostrate king, whose crown has been cast down before
the Almighty, the Everlasting One says, 'I have found me
a man after mine own heart, who shall fulfill my will.' To
which the monarch replies, 'Thy word is a lantern unto
my feet.' In this imaginary message to Henry, one notes
the flattery of Hans Holbein more than the pronouncement
of the Eternal. The rest of the frontispiece is more factual.
Seated on a throne, the king holds in each hand a Bible
marked *Verbum Dei*. One he hands to Cranmer and the
other to Cromwell. To Cranmer the king says, 'Take this
and teach'; to Cromwell, 'I make a decree that in all my
kingdom men shall tremble and fear before the Living God.'
Beneath the monarch's feet, a scroll bears a message ap-

plying to king as well as to people, prelates, and officials: 'Judge righteous judgment; turn not away your ear from the prayer of any poor man.' In gratitude for the gift of the open Bible, the people are pictured as crying out, '*Vivat Rex*,' and 'God save the king.'

It was a great day. An authorized Bible in the vernacular had been granted free passage throughout the land; the people had been given permission to read it without molestation. A few years later, observing how men turned its content to serve their peculiar purpose, Cranmer composed a prayer to be said by those who heard or read the Holy Scriptures:

> Blessed Lord, who hast caused all holy Scriptures to be written for our learning; Grant that we may in such wise hear them, read, mark, learn, and inwardly digest them, that by patience and comfort of thy Holy Word, we may embrace, and ever hold fast, the blessed hope of everlasting life, which thou hast given us in our Saviour Jesus Christ. *Amen.*

This prayer, first inserted in the Book of 1549, has remained in each succeeding revision.

In 1540, at the insistence of Cranmer, Convocation appointed a committee of eight to reform the service books, thus making a real beginning in liturgical reformation and enrichment. The committee seems to have continued through successive Convocations and to have been reappointed in the reign of Edward VI. In 1540 a revised Psalter in Latin and English was printed by Richard Grafton. Cranmer informed Convocation in 1542 that it was the king's will that the service books be more thoroughly reformed, that the pope's name be deleted, and that, among other things, the names of saints not mentioned in the Holy Scripture or in 'authentical doctors' be removed. The revision was made, and the Sarum

Rite was required throughout the province of Canterbury. According to Dom Gasquet, Cranmer appeared again before Convocation, this time in 1543, demanding more drastic reformation on the ground that it was the royal will that

> all mass books, antiphoners, portasses, in the church of England should be newly examined, reformed, and castigated from all manner of mention of the bishop of Rome's name; from all apocryphas, feigned legends, superstitious orations, collects, versicles and responses: that the names and memories of all saints which were not contained in the Scripture or authentic doctors should be abolished and put out of the same books and calendars and that the service should be made out of the Scriptures and other authentic doctors.[4]

The Convocation directed that in every church after the Te Deum and the Magnificat a lesson should be read from the New Testament, and when that had been completed then one should be read from the Old Testament.

Dom Gasquet, in his *Edward VI and the Book of Common Prayer*, believed the reformation committee appointed by the upper house of Convocation did not serve, since he was unable to find evidence of its ratification by the lower house; but events indicate otherwise, for more liturgical work directed toward reformation was accomplished than published or generally revealed. Important studies were made of existing and newly created services. It is almost beyond dispute that the revision committee, under the leadership of Archbishop Cranmer, worked hard at the task of preparing a vernacular service, and that discord among parties in the Church, and the attitude of Henry, prevented much liturgical revision from being placed before

[4] Francis Aidan Gasquet, O.S.B., and Edmund Bishop, *Edward VI and the Book of Common Prayer* (London: John Hodges, 1890), p. 27.

Convocation.[5] Evidence of the work of the 1540 committee of revision is found in the request of the members of
the lower house of Convocation (which met in St. Paul's,
London, November 4, 1547, in the first year of Edward
VI) that 'the labors of the bishops and others who by
command of convocation had been engaged in examining,
revising, and setting forth (*et edendo*) the divine service
should be produced and should be submitted to the examination of this house.'[6] The notes of Archbishop
Cranmer show, according to Dom Gasquet, that 'by command of King Henry VIII certain prelates and learned
men were appointed . . . . to devise a uniform order;
who according to the same appointment *did make certain
books*, as they be informed.'[7] There is no contradiction
here between the two statements. Convocation, having
acknowledged the supreme authority of the king, could
make no appointment of a liturgical committee apart from
the royal will. Both Convocation and Cranmer were correct; the committee was appointed, and produced results,
published and unpublished.

One of the published results was the Litany of 1544. A
skillful piece of liturgical revision and enrichment, this
service, which was issued by royal authority, has stood
the test of over four hundred years of devotional use. It
was composed of the old Sarum Litany and other material. In 1544 the Sarum Litany was revised in the light
of Luther's Litany of 1525, the Consultations of Hermann, and the opinions of Cranmer and his associates. A
copy of the 1544 Litany may be found in Henrician form
in the *Private Prayers of the Reign of Queen Elizabeth*.
The pre-reformation litany, of which this was a revision,
like the Roman Catholic litany, contained a list of saints,

[5] A similar attitude on the part of many persons long delayed the 1892
revision and enrichment of the American Book of Common Prayer
[6] Gasquet and Bishop, *op. cit.*, p. 1.
[7] *Ibid.*

each followed by the petition, 'Pray for us.' In revising
the litany for publication in English, Cranmer and his
fellow liturgists, avoided what might be considered vain
repetition by summing up all these petitions in three. As
revised, the litany opened as the American Book did before the 1928 revision. Following the invocation of the
Blessed Trinity, it contained an invocation of the Blessed
Virgin, another of the holy angels, archangels, and all the
orders of blessed spirits; then an invocation of the holy
patriarchs, apostles, martyrs, confessors, and virgins, and
all the blessed company of heaven, who were requested to
pray for the petitioners. The litany then continued much
as today, save for the prayer for deliverance from 'the
bishop of Rome and all his detestable enormities.' This
petition, inserted in Henry's time, was removed in the time
of Queen Elizabeth. Two petitions for the king's protec-
tion appear in the litany, placed there because of the wars
with France and Scotland. One read, 'That it may please
thee to be his defender and keeper, giving him victory over
all his enemies.' The service ended with the Prayer of St.
Chrysostom, showing that the revisers were familiar with
the liturgy bearing that name.

This 1544 English Litany was one of several processions
revised, translated, or created by Cranmer and his assistants,
but it was the only one Henry VIII would permit to be
published and used. That there were others is clear from
Archbishop Cranmer's letter to King Henry VIII, dated
October 7, 1544:

> It may please your Majesty to be advertised, that, accord-
> ing to your Highness' commandment, sent unto me by
> your Grace's Secretary, Mr. Pagett, I have translated
> into the English tongue, so well as I could in so short a
> time, certain processions to be used on festival days, if
> after due correction and amendment of the same, your

Highness shall think so convenient. In which translation, forasmuch as many of the processions, in the Latin, were but barren, as me seemed, and little fruitful, I was constrained to use more than the liberty of a translator: for in some processions I have altered divers words; in some I have added part; in some taken part away; some I have left out whole, either for bycause the matter appeared to me to be to little purpose, or bycause the days be not with us festival days [having been abrogated in 1537]; and some processions I have added whole, because I thought I had better matter for the purpose than was the procession in Latin; the judgment whereof I leave wholly unto your Majesty: and after your Highness hath corrected it, if your Grace command some devout and solemn note to be made thereunto (as is to the procession which your Majesty hath already set forth in English), I trust it will much excitate and stir the hearts of all men unto devotion and godliness. But in mine own opinion, the song that shall be made thereunto should not be full of notes, but as near as may be for every syllable a note; so that it may be sung distinctly and devoutly as be the Matins and Evensong, Venite, the Hymns, Te Deum, Benedictus, Magnificat, Nunc Dimittis, and all the Psalms and Versicles; and in the Mass, Gloria in Excelsis, Gloria Patri, the Creed, the Preface, the Pater Noster, and some of the Sanctus and Agnus. As concerning the Salve Festa Dies, the Latin note, as I think, is sober and distinct enough; wherefore I have travailed to make the verses in English and have put the Latin note in the same. Nevertheless, they that be cunning in singing, can make a much more solemn note thereto. I made them only for a proof, to see how English would do in song. But bycause mine English verses lack the grace and facility that I would wish they had, your Majesty may cause some other to make them again, that can do the same in more pleasant English and phrase.

As for the sentence [sense], I suppose it will serve well enough. Thus Almighty God preserve your Majesty in long and prosperous health and felicity. From Bekisbourne, the 7th of October. Your Grace's most bounden Chaplain and Beadsman. T. Cantuarien.[8]

The significance of this letter is clear. King Henry had requested that several processions (litanies or like services) be revised and submitted to him for judgment and authorization. One he accepted and authorized, and to his action we owe our present Litany. The others he refused to authorize or allow published. What were they like? Where are they today? By his refusal of permission for publication the Church may have lost one or more of its most priceless heritages. Here in America we can only wonder, but in England fruitful search might be made even at this late date.

Entrusted by the king and Convocation with the revision of the service books, the Archbishop and his assistants did more than review and issue the Breviary and the Latin Mass, more than revise and compose processionals, more than reform and issue the Litany of 1544; for they also studied the whole matter of producing a vernacular service for the Church of England. Dom Gasquet discovered in the eighteen-eighties a manuscript which shows conclusively that Archbishop Cranmer and others were at work on the production of a revised breviary and a service of Morning and Evening Prayer; and the fact that before his death Henry VIII instructed Cranmer to 'pen a form for the alteration of the Mass into a Communion' shows that the king had more of a hand in the liturgical preparation for the 1549 Book of Common Prayer than is commonly supposed.

The contribution made during the long reign of Henry VIII to the liturgical reformation in the Church of Eng-

[8] John Henry Blunt, *The Annotated Book of Common Prayer* (London: Rivington's, 1866), pp. XXII-XXIII.

land, and to the preparation of the Book of Common Prayer, may be summed up thus: he authorized the revision of the old service books, the mass books, and the publication of the Primer in English; he authorized the translation and publication of the Great Bible, and its use in the Churches; by the Royal Supremacy Act, he united under the royal, rather than the papal, authority the two historic sections of the Church of England, the Convocations of York and Canterbury; he derived from Convocation through the offices of Archbishop Warham the admission that the king, and not the pope, was the supreme head in earth of the Church of England, so far as the law of Christ will allow; he led Parliament in repudiation of papal sovereignty over the English nation and the patriarchal sees of York and Canterbury; he permitted the publication of an English Psalter and a book of Epistles and Gospels in English; he approved convocational direction that the Bible be read in English after the Te Deum and the Magnificat; by his direction, the Breviary and mass books were pruned of all reference to the bishop of Rome and the papacy and superstition; he granted license as royal printers to Grafton and Whitchurche and directed that no liturgical books be printed by unlicensed persons in England or purchased from abroad, thus freeing the Church of England from dependence on foreign publishers for its liturgical equipment; he directed Cranmer and a committee of prelates and divines to labor at the revision of the services with a view to their being turned into the vernacular; and before his death he directed the Archbishop of Canterbury to begin transforming the mass into a communion. Thus, in spite of his sinfulness, Henry VIII did much for the advancement of the worship of God, in England and beyond, by his liturgical preparation for the work which was later accomplished under his son Edward and his daughter Elizabeth.

CHAPTER III

FROM THE 1549 TO THE 1662 BOOK

Edward vi succeeded his father King Henry on January 28, 1547. Edward was precocious and pious. His father saw to it that he was educated in the new learning and indoctrinated with the reforming spirit. Drastic alterations appeared at once in the public worship of the Church. In April Compline was sung in the vernacular in the Chapel Royal; in July the Book of Homilies was issued and ordered read in public worship; in August the Injunctions of Edward required that the English Bible be read at Matins and Evensong and that the clergy obtain the Paraphrases of Erasmus, study them, and read them to their people. The Epistle and Gospel were ordered read in English at High Mass, and the services of Matins and Evensong were allowed in shortened form when a sermon was preached.

Parliament, which met concurrently with Convocation, was opened November 4, 1547, by a celebration of High Mass during which the Gloria in Excelsis, the Credo, and the Agnus were sung in English. The lower house of Convocation, through its spokesman, requested the upper house to place before it the result of the liturgical work formerly considered or accomplished by Archbishop Cranmer and his assistants. That the work was carried on is evidenced by the Order for Communion and the Latin manuscript

(Royal Ms. 7. B. IV) discovered in 1888. In the reign of Henry VIII, himself a brilliant theologian and scholar, Cranmer worked on a revision of the Calendar and the transformation of the Breviary into a more practical manual of worship. Royal Ms. 7. B. IV has been proved Cranmer's workmanship; some of it is in his own writing and some, in the writing of his known scribe, is corrected in the writing of Cranmer. This document, a folio manuscript of one hundred fifty-nine pages, contains the Archbishop's attempted construction of a scheme for daily reading of Holy Scripture and two plans for breviary alteration.

Of special interest is Cranmer's second plan, whereby the traditional offices were to be reduced to two, Matins and Vespers. In this plan Archbishop Cranmer and his associates moved from the old Sarum system of breviary worship to the Prayer Book method of Morning and Evening Prayer. The manuscript is important because it shows how the members of the Windsor Revision Committee, under the guidance of the scholarly but cautious Cranmer, thought their way out of the complex impracticality of the Latin Breviary into the reasoned simplicity of the Book of Common Prayer. The plan served as a connecting link between the revised Latin Breviary of Henry VIII and the 1549 services of Matins and Evensong. If the preface to Quignon's Reformed Breviary, the preface of Cranmer's Proposed Revision in Royal Ms. 7. B. IV, and the Preface of the 1549 Book of Common Prayer are placed side by side in the order mentioned, it becomes evident that the 1549 Preface was derived in part from the Latin preface in Royal Ms. 7. B. IV, which in turn was derived in part from the preface of the Reformed Breviary of Cardinal Quignon. A comparison of the skeleton of the second proposed plan of breviary revision in R. Ms. 7. B. IV and the 1549 service of Matins will show their close relationship.

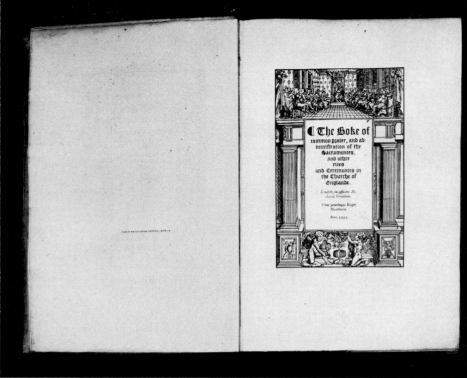

Photo by T. Horydczak, Washington

THE 1559 BOOK OF COMMON PRAYER, TITLE PAGE—a Pickering reprint of an edition originally printed by Richard Grafton, Printer to the Queen's Majesty. The pages measure 9 by 14 inches. Queen Elizabeth, as Supreme Governor of All Causes Spiritual and Temporal, appointed Matthew Parker, Edmund Grindall, James Pilkington, Richard Cox, William May, William Bill, Sir Thomas Smith, David Whitehead, Edwin Sandys, and Edmund Guest to prepare a Book of Common Prayer. Though the queen desired the restoration of the Book of 1549, revised to meet conditions prevailing in her day, the committee employed as the basis of its revision the 1552 Book and occasionally referred to the earlier edition. The 1559 Book was comprehensive; it combined the Sentences of Administration of Holy Communion found in the Books of 1549 and 1552—a combination which has been continued in all subsequent editions. This Book, as determined upon by the committee and affixed to the Act of Uniformity, became law on April 28, 1559, and, with the authority of Parliament and the queen, was ordered in use on St. John the Baptist's Day, June 24, 1559. Two members of the committee, William May and Richard Cox, having served on the original committee of 1549, constituted living links between editions. The book illustrated here is in the Washington Cathedral Library.

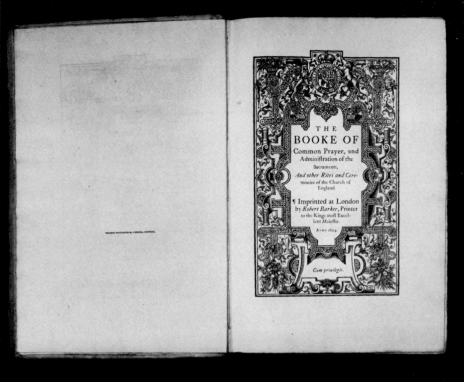

THE

BOOKE OF

Common Prayer, and
Adminiſtration of the
Sacraments,
And other Rites and Cere-
monies of the Church of
England.

¶ Imprinted at London
by *Robert Barker*, Printer
to the Kings moſt Excel-
lent Maieſtie.

ANNO 1604.

Cum priuilegio.

THE 1604 BOOK OF COMMON PRAYER, TITLE PAGE—a Pickering reprint of
an edition originally published in London by Robert Barker, printer
to the King's Most Excellent Majesty. The pages measure 9 by 14 inches.
The 1604 Book, set forth by James I, is a slightly revised version of the
1559 Book, having been altered in the light of the Hampton Court Conference of 1603-4. The conference resulted in a royal directive to the
bishops to amend the Book in accordance with alterations specified by
the king. As amended the Book was not set forth with the authority of
Convocation or of Parliament; it was issued by royal authority under
the unspecified power resident in the crown and was set forth not as a
new Book but as the 1559 Book corrected 'by explanations.' Issued under
a clause in the Elizabethan Act of Uniformity which empowered the
crown to issue orders concerning ceremonies being abused, it continued
in use until 1645. The most important difference between this and the
1559 Book is the addition of the sacramental portion of the Catechism,
written by John Overall, then Dean of St. Paul's, London, and in 1614
Bishop of Coventry. In all probability this amended edition of the Book
of Common Prayer was that used at James Town, Virginia, in the first
celebration of the Holy Communion conducted there by the Rev. Robert
Hunt on June 21, 1607; and also by the Rev. Richard Seymour at Monhegan Island on August 9, 1607. The volume illustrated on this page is in
Washington Cathedral Library.

PROPOSED SERVICE OF MATINS [1]	MATINS IN BOOK OF 1549 [1]
(Outline derived from the Third Appendix [Latin] of *Edward VI and the Book of Common Prayer* by Francis Aiden Gasquet and Edmund Bishop, p. 31, and Appendix III, pp. 374-375.)	(Outline derived from Matins in the 1549 Book of Common Prayer, which was published by Richard Grafton and Edward Whitchurche of London in 1549.)

1. The Lord's Prayer	1. The Lord's Prayer
2. The Versicles	2. The Versicles
3. The Gloria Patri, or Alleluia	3. The Gloria Patri, and Praise Ye the Lord
4. Praise be to Thee, O Lord, etc. (From Septuagesima to Easter)	4. Alleluia (From Easter to Trinity Sunday)
5.	5. The Venite
6. Hymn	6. ....
7. Three Psalms, Gloria Patri after each Psalm	7. The Psalms, Gloria Patri after each Psalm
The Book of Psalms to be read through monthly and the Venite simply to be used in its turn as a Psalm.	The Psalms to be read through monthly, as required by the table, or Proper Psalms to be read if such are appointed.
8. The Lord's Prayer	8. ....
9. Three Lessons. Each preceded by a request for the officiant's blessing, and each followed by an ascription.	9. Two Lessons. One from the Old Testament and the other from the New. The blessing and ascription are omitted but the Lessons are announced and ended as is the present custom. The First Lesson is followed by the Te Deum or Benedicite and the Second Lesson is followed by the Benedictus.
10. The Te Deum	10. ....
11.	11. The Shorter Kyrie
12. A Fourth Lesson on Sundays or special occasions. To be read from the Homily or from a history of the Saints.	12. ....

[1] Provision was made for shortening this service whenever a sermon was preached.

Proposed Service of Matins [1]	Matins in Book of 1549 [1]
13. Benedictus and Gloria Patri	13. ....
14.	14. The Apostles' Creed
15.	15. The Lord's Prayer
16. The Versicles	16. The Versicles
17. The Collect	17. ....
18. Versicles	18. ....
19. The Athanasian Creed	19. ....
20. Versicles (not the same as in the 1549 Book)	20. Versicles
21.	21. The Collect for the Day
22.	22. The Collect for Peace
23. The Collect for Grace	23. The Collect for Grace
24. Versicles	24. ....

Thus it is plain how Archbishop Cranmer and other members of the 1549 revision committee worked from the reformed Breviary to the 1549 Matins. In the proposed service Cranmer adopted the calendar year rather than the ecclesiastical for regulating the reading of the lessons from Holy Scripture. The same procedure was followed in the first Book of Common Prayer and carried out Cardinal Quignon's proposal that nothing be permitted to interfere with continuous reading of Holy Scripture. Obviously this manuscript is one of the documents the lower house of Convocation desired to examine.

In December, 1547, Convocation agreed without vocal objection that the sacrament of Holy Communion should be administered in both kinds. While this agreement was being reached in Convocation, legislation was being pushed through Parliament to make the proposal into law. As soon as the Act for the Communion in Both Kinds, restoring the cup to the laity, was passed, the bishops assembled for deliberation on how to implement the parliamentary legislation. The result was the Order for the Communion, published by the Royal Printer, Richard Grafton, on March 8, 1548, and ordered into use on Easter, April 1, 1548. This

[1] *Ibid.*

was not a service for the celebration of Holy Communion
but merely a form for the administration of the sacred elements after they had been consecrated by use of the Sarum
Mass. To this mass, it was ordered attached immediately
after the celebrant's communion. The substance of the
rite was taken from the Consultations of Hermann, the
Lutheran-minded excommunicated Roman Catholic Archbishop of Cologne, and contained an announcement of,
and an exhortation to, a future communion; an exhortation
to be said at the time of the celebration of communion; an
exhortation to those intending to receive the communion;
a general confession; an absolution; comfortable words; a
prayer of humble access; words of administration of the
sacred elements; and the first portion of the present bene-
diction in the Holy Communion. All of this rite except the
King's Preface found its way into the Book of Common
Prayer. It now forms a vital part of the service of Holy
Communion. The publication of this service of administration without the other portions necessary for a full
celebration suggests that the bishops and the archbishop
were reserving judgment on a plan which originated in the
days of Henry VIII and which, because of difference of
opinion, was at the moment impossible of completion.

Soon after the Order for Communion was put into general use the Church was ready for the appearance in the
vernacular of a complete service of Holy Communion. The
King's Preface to the Order for Communion promised
additional revision of the services of the Church, and that
promise was fulfilled in 1548 by a committee consisting
almost certainly of Thomas Cranmer, Archbishop of
Canterbury and master of musical prose; Thomas Good-
rich, Bishop of Ely and author of the first half of our Catechism; Henry Holbech, Bishop of Lincoln, ex-Benedic-
tine monk, who exchanged the vows of holy celibacy for
those of holy matrimony; George Day, Bishop of Chich-

ester, a conservative Etonian who refused to pull down the altars and replace them by tables; John Skip, Bishop of Hereford, almoner to Anne Boleyn and ex-abbot of Wigmore; Thomas Thirlby, first and last Bishop of Westminster, under Mary appointed 'degrader,' with the sadistic Bonner, of the rejected and tortured Cranmer; and Nicholas Ridley, Bishop of Rochester, wise of counsel and apt at chess. Other members of the committee were William May, Dean of St. Paul's, London, canonist and member of the committee which produced the *Reformatio Legum;* Richard Cox, Dean of Christ Church and chancellor of the University of Oxford; John Taylor, Dean of Lincoln, deprived under Queen Mary for his anti-papal opinions; Simon Heynes, Dean of Exeter, of whom little is known; Thomas Robertson, Archdeacon of Leicester, who, having conformed under Mary, was rewarded with an episcopate; and John Redmayne, the moderate-minded master of Trinity College, Cambridge. The coats-of-arms of the dioceses of many of these men appear in the Prayer Book window in Washington Cathedral.

These were the men who assembled at Windsor, and perhaps from time to time at Chertsey, to create the first Book of Common Prayer. They had before them, or were at least acquainted with, the Reformed Breviary of Henry VIII, the Processionals, the 1544 Litany, the Primer of 1545, the Book of the Gospels and Epistles, the *Book of Godly Prayers*, the Great Bible, the Royal Ms. 7. B. IV, the Order of Communion, the Consultations of Hermann, and the Reformed Breviary of Cardinal Quignon. On Christmas Day, 1548, they finished the Book of Common Prayer. Parliament passed the Act of Uniformity, with the Book attached, on January 21, 1549, and ordered the Book put in use on and after Whitsunday, June 9, 1549. In order that the Book should remain within the financial reach of all, price-control was imposed, and no one was permitted to charge more than the price set by order of the king.

The authorization and publication of the first Book of Common Prayer was a turning-point in liturgical history. For the first time English churchmen had in their own language a Book of Common Prayer, containing all the needed parts of the services. It was a book which, purged of superstition, was Biblical, patristic, and systematic. Its content was similar to that of our present Book, but it lacked the enrichments which have been added during the centuries. Characteristic of it were the reduction of the numerous breviary services to two, Matins and Evensong; the deletion of all mention of the Bishop of Rome's previously exercised authority; the use of the Apostles' Creed at Matins and the Athanasian Creed on stated occasions; the revision of the Sarum Mass and the addition to it of portions from the Consultations of Hermann; the permission of reservation of the consecrated elements for the sick and the prohibition of the elevation of the consecrated host for eucharistic adoration; and, above all, the systematic revision and arrangement of the services of the Church in the spirit of sane Biblical and patristic Catholicism.

Not everybody liked the Book. Even though in the interest of unity all the creating committee accepted it, men like the astute Gardiner and the brutal Bonner disliked it because of its lack of clear-cut statements favoring their positions. The foreigners Martyr, Bucer and à Lasco despised it. Cranmer may or may not have been satisfied with the Book. At any rate a careful study of the parties of the period leads to the assumption that there was dissension in the committee, with Gardiner on one side and Cranmer on the other. In 1550 the latter wrote *A Defence of the True and Catholic Doctrine of the Holy Communion,* supporting the reformed doctrine of the sacrament. In this book he abandoned as non-Catholic and non-Biblical the doctrine of transubstantiation—a theory which theologians had propounded as an application of Aristotle's concept of substance and accidents, and which had been widely accepted throughout Western Catholicism.

The Book of 1549 was doomed to alteration. Its revision was undertaken in 1552. The Book, as revised, was ordered by the Second Act of Uniformity to be used throughout the Church on and after All Saints' Day, November 1, 1552. Protestant as it was, the foreign reformers were disappointed in it, and opposed it. Martin Bucer, the Lutheran, who may have been the author of the General Confession, attacked it; Peter Martyr, the Italian, wanted its sacramental tone lowered; and à Lasco, the Pole, wanted nothing to do with it. These and all who joined with them exhausted the patience of the well-intended and over-taxed archbishop, who wrote to the king,

> I trust ye will not be moved with these glorious and unquiet spirits which can like nothing but that is after their own fancy; and cease not to make trouble when things be most quiet and in good order, if such men should be heard, although the book were made every year anew, yet it should not lack faults in their opinion.[2]

In some ways the Book of 1552 was an improvement over that of 1549, but in others it was an impoverishment. The desirable features were the addition of an introductory part to Morning and Evening Prayer, consisting of the Sentences, Exhortation, General Confession and Absolution; the elimination of the word 'mass' from the title of the Order for the Administration of the Lord's Supper or Holy Communion; the purification of the service of Holy Baptism by the removal of the alleged exorcism of the devil or evil spirits from unbaptized babies; and the relocation of the Gloria in Excelsis. On the other hand the

[2] Blunt, op. cit., p. XXXI.

1552 Book of Common Prayer was weakened by the deletion of the Invocation of the Holy Spirit in the Prayer of Consecration; the impersonalization of the Office for the Burial of the Dead by the removal of prayers for the departed; the omission of unction from the Visitation of the Sick; the removal of permission to reserve enough of the sacrament for communicating the sick; and the elimination of the Agnus Dei from the service of Holy Communion.

In the reign of Mary, daughter of Henry VIII and Catherine of Aragon, the 1552 Book was considered legal until a sufficient number of Latin service books could be obtained. After December 20, 1553, it was no longer allowed. Mary's first Act of Repeal shifted the liturgical status of the Church of England back to that of the year 1529, but the reaction did not continue long. In November, 1558, Elizabeth came to the throne. By her wise and far-seeing administration, she stabilized the political and liturgical reorganization of English civil and ecclesiastical life.

Three parties faced Elizabeth on her accession to the throne—one a large pro-Roman group mostly in the North and West; one a large pro-Protestant group, created as much by the horror of Mary's burning of 'heretics' as by personal conviction on the part of exiles returned from the Continent; and a third composed of English churchmen suspicious of both Rome and Geneva. The queen allied herself, actually, to the latter group, but she waited some time before she made any move toward changing the liturgical situation. Then, on December 27, 1558, in the interest of harmony, she issued a proclamation prohibiting preaching. She refused the title, Supreme Head of the Church of England, but accepted that of Supreme Governor in all Causes Spiritual as well as Temporal. Acting as such, she appointed a committee—Matthew Parker (later Archbishop of Canterbury), Edmund Grindal, James Pilkington, Richard Cox, William May, William Bill, Sir

Thomas Smith, David Whitehead, Edwin Sandys, and Edmund Guest. The committee met in the home of the queen's secretary, Sir Thomas Smith, and at his suggestion.

It was an irregular committee, formed not by direction of Convocation or of Parliament but by the queen's command. It studied the 1552 Book of Common Prayer and recommended alterations which Parliament adopted. Annexed to the Act of Uniformity, the Book became law on April 28, 1559. It came into use with the authority of the queen and of Parliament, but without the authorization of Convocation. Parliament ordered the Book of 1559 used on and after St. John the Baptist's Day, June 24, 1559. Two of the committee, William May and Richard Cox, were members of the original group which produced the 1549 Book.

The Book of 1559 is of interest to Americans not only because it is one of the liturgical links in the evolution of the American Book but also because it was used at the baptism of Manteo and Virginia Dare on Roanoke Island. That it was an effort at comprehension is seen in the combination of the 1549 and 1552 Sentences of Administration of the consecrated elements in the Holy Communion. The 1549 sentence used at the administration of the consecrated bread was 'The body of our Lorde Jesus Christe whiche was geuen for thee, preserue thy bodye and soule unto euerlasting lyfe.' The 1552 sentence read, 'Take and eate this, in remembraunce that Christ dyed for thee, and feede on him in thy hearte by faythe, with thankesgeuing.' These were added together in the 1559 revision and made to read as follows: 'The bodie of our Lord Jesu Christ, which was geuen for thee, preserue thy body and soule into euerlasting life: and take and ete this in remembraunce that Christ died for thee, feede on him in thine heart by faith, with thankesgeuynge.' What was done with the 1549 and 1552 Sentences of Administration of the consecrated bread was also done with the sentences used in connection with the administration of the wine. These combinations of diverse sentences show the spirit of comprehension which animated the revisers of the Book of 1559. It was the most inspired feature of their work. It illustrates the theological fact that divine truth is often revealed by 'both and' rather than by 'either or.'

In addition to combining the Sentences of Administration, the 1559 Book removed from the Litany the petition for deliverance from the 'detestable enormities' of the Bishop of Rome; added the Ornaments Rubric, which authorized a return of such vestments as were in use in the second year of Edward VI; and omitted the 'Black Rubric' concerning kneeling at communion. The 1559 Book met general acceptance. Of the 9,400 clergy then exercising their ministry in the Church of England, less than 200 refused to use it.

The next Book of Common Prayer, that of 1604, was issued in the reign of James I, who succeeded Elizabeth. As a result of the Hampton Court Conference of 1603-4, called by King James I to hear the grievances of the signers of the Millenary Petition (so named because of its pretended one thousand signatures), the Book of Common Prayer was set forth by royal authority. This was a slight revision of the Book of 1559; to all intents and purposes it was the same one. The only important changes made were 'or remission of sins' added to the title of the Absolution, a prayer for the royal family placed at the end of the Litany, a few thanksgivings, and the addition of Dean Overall's sacramental section at the end of the Catechism.

The Cromwellian Interregnum, which followed the execution of Charles I and William Laud, overthrew the Church of England, abolished the Book of 1604, and set up in its place the *Directory of Worship*. When the chaos of the Interregnum became more than the 'presbyterian' clergy and laymen of the Church of England could endure, they joined cause with the royalists, overthrew the Commonwealth with its Protectorate, and restored the monarchy under parliamentary limitations—actions which, to the disappointment of the presbyterians, carried with them the restoration of episcopal government and the Book of Common Prayer.

The political and ecclesiastical turmoils of the sixteenth and seventeenth centuries in England, in spite of their immediate pain to those concerned, proved an enduring blessing to England and to all English-speaking people. England and America are indebted to Henry VIII for the revelation that sovereignty is indivisible, that part cannot be exercised within a nation and part of it from outside its borders. Under the reigns of the four Stuarts—reigns which were interrupted by the Interregnum—it became established that the people have a right to representative government and that public officials, hereditary or elected, rule by sufferance of the people and under the law. This fact Oliver Cromwell taught England and the world.

Oliver Cromwell was a complex personality, stern and austere in his public life, and yet a man of some breadth of spirit. He at times could advocate freedom of conscience and religious worship (for all save Anglicans, Roman Catholics, and Unitarians—and, as far as he dared, for Jews). In his private life kindly and genial, he was sincere in believing that peace could come to English life only by the obliteration of prelacy, which to him was identical with episcopacy. The presbyterian clergy of the Church of England looked to him with high hopes. These clergy were men like Edward Reynolds, author of our General Thanksgiving, who believed that ordination of a presbyter by a college of presbyters was as valid as ordination by a bishop and presbyters. Hence they desired the presbyterianization of the government of the Church of England and the liberalization of its services of worship. They were amazed to find, as time went on, that Cromwell seemed to favor independency rather than presbyterian or episcopal church government and, when the time came during the administration of Oliver Cromwell's son, they joined cause with the royalists in overthrowing the Commonwealth.

As a result of the leadership of General Monk, the Commonwealth was overthrown and the monarchy re-established, subject to the directives of Parliament. Charles II was met at Breda by a delegation of the presbyterian clergy who requested that the surplice be not worn during worship and that the Book of Common Prayer be not restored. The king promised toleration and agreed to call a conference at which he would hear the opinions of the opponents of the Book of Common Prayer. March 25, 1661, he issued a royal commission to the returned bishops of the Church and the presbyterian Church of England clergy, instructing them to assemble at the Savoy, the Bishop of London's palace in the Strand, to consider the liturgical needs of the Church. The commission opened April 15, 1661, and continued in session until July 24. The Church of England was represented by Accepted Frewen, Archbishop of York, and eleven bishops as principals, among whom were John Cosin, Bishop of Durham and author of many of the Collects and prayers inserted in the 1662 Book of Common Prayer, John Gauden, and nine coadjutors. Among the latter were Peter Gunning, author of the Prayer for All Conditions of Men, and John Pearson, author of *An Exposition of the Creed*, a masterly theological work little known today. The presbyterians were represented by Edward Reynolds, Bishop of Norwich, eleven presbyters as principals, and nine presbyters as coadjutors. The presbyterians presented a long list of objections to the Book of Common Prayer as it existed in the latter years of Charles I. Some objections were trivial and others had real merit. Many were accepted by the episcopal side of the commission; others have since found their way into the American Book of Common Prayer. A strange request of the presbyterian group was for the abandonment of the ring in marriage. One wonders what they would say about the use today of two rings in many Protestant marriage services.

The Book of 1662 was adopted in Convocation as a result of the action taken by the bishops at the Savoy. Much of the revision and enrichment was the work of Bishop Cosin, whose own annotated Durham Prayer Book furnished liturgical wisdom to the revising committee. The Book was ratified by Parliament, granted royal assent April 19, 1662, and by Act of Parliament made the official Book of the Church of England and ordered in use on St. Bartholomew's Day, August 24. In spite of attempts to alter it, this Book has remained the official Book of Common Prayer of the Church of England. It was the Book used by the Church of England in the American Colonies during the American Revolution. It is the Book used in England today.

The outstanding characteristics which distinguish it from the Book of 1559 are:

1. The enlargement of the last part of Morning and Evening Prayer.
2. The revision of the Litany by the incorporation of petitions for deliverance from schism and rebellion.
3. The reinsertion of the 'Black Rubric'; in the place of the phrase, 'real and essential presence'; the words 'any corporeal presence' were used to disapprove of eucharistic adoration.
4. The inclusion of the service for the Ministration of Holy Baptism to Adults in order to provide for those who had not been baptized during the Interregnum,

and for savages who had been converted to Christ in the colonies.

5. The changing of the word 'minister' to the word 'priest' in the rubric preceding the Absolution, and the phrase 'Bishops, Pastors, and Ministers' to 'Bishops, Priests, and Deacons.'

6. The incorporation of Bishop Peter Gunning's great Prayer for All Conditions of Men in Morning and Evening Prayer; and the incorporation of the General Thanksgiving written by Bishop Edward Reynolds, leader of the presbyterian clergy at the conference of the Savoy.

7. The authorization of the use of the text of the King James Version of the Bible for the Epistles and Gospels and for many of the Lessons of Morning and Evening Prayer.

8. The addition of A Form of Prayer to be Used at Sea —a tribute to England's expanding naval might.

9. The alteration of the Preface to the Ordinal to assert the requirement of episcopal ordination for those who minister at the altars of the Church of England.

CHAPTER IV

THE AMERICAN BOOK OF COMMON PRAYER

AFTER THE American Revolution, conventions were held in the various states and plans for liturgical revision were determined upon. These were brought before the 'Convention of the Protestant Episcopal Church in the states of New York, New Jersey, Pennsylvania, Delaware, Maryland, Virginia and South Carolina, held in Christ Church, in the City of Philadelphia, from September 27 to October 7, 1785.'[1] This convention, as reported in its journal, adopted a resolution calling for the appointment of a committee:

[consisting of] one Clerical and one Lay deputy from each state, to consider of and report such alterations in the Liturgy, as shall render it consistent with the American revolution, and the constitutions of the respective states: And such further alterations in the Liturgy, as it may be advisable for this Convention to recommend to the consideration of the Church here represented.[2]

The revision committee was a sub-committee of a larger group chosen to draft an ecclesiastical constitution for the Protestant Episcopal Church in the United States of

---

[1] *Journals of General Convention from 1784 to 1814* (Philadelphia: John Bioren, 1817), *Convention of 1785*, p. B.
[2] *Ibid.*, p. 5.

America. The Rev. William Smith, D.D., was made chairman of the committee to prepare a Book of Common Prayer. After the General Convention had adopted the Proposed Book, it set up a committee, under the chairmanship of the Rev. Charles Wharton and the Rev. William Smith, to edit and publish it, and, after all expenses were paid, to remit the 'nett profits to the Treasurers of the several Corporations and Societies for the relief of the widows and children of deceased Clergymen in the states represented in this Convention; the profits to be equally divided among the said Societies and Corporations.' [3] This Proposed Book, adopted in 1785, and published in 1786 by Hall and Sellers, went into an edition of four thousand copies. Sheets were sent to England by the editing committee, and the book was reprinted there by J. Debrett. Fifty copies of the reprint were made for the bishops of the Church of England, who were considering consecrating bishops for the American Church.

No sooner was the Proposed Book off the press in America and reprinted in England than it met with a storm of objection. The thoroughly dissatisfied English bishops expressed themselves as unable to grant the American request for the gift of the episcopate until they were assured certain corrections would be made and the American Church would not depart from the substance of the Faith in such manner as the Proposed Book seemed to indicate. Some of the English objections were based on the omission of the Nicene and Athanasian Creeds and of the 'Descent into Hell' phrase in the Apostles' Creed.

Through its corresponding committee, the American Church convinced the English bishops that every effort would be made to restore the Nicene Creed and to keep the American Church in harmony with the Doctrine and Worship of the Church of England. In due time, and with

[3] *Ibid.*

the assistance of our ambassador to the Court of St. James's, Parliament was persuaded to pass an enabling act permitting the English bishops to consecrate to the episcopate men who were not subjects of the British crown and who would not minister in British dominions. Under this Act, the Rev. William White and the Rev. Samuel Provoost were consecrated bishops in the chapel of Lambeth Palace on February 4, 1787.

When the two American bishops returned from England, General Convention assembled in Christ Church, Philadelphia, on Tuesday, July 28, 1789. The dioceses of New York, New Jersey, Pennsylvania, Delaware, Maryland, Virginia, and South Carolina were represented. Bishop Seabury of Connecticut was absent, having misinterpreted a resolution of a previous convention as declaring invalid his Scottish non-juring orders. A resolution was unanimously passed 'That it is the opinion of this Convention, that the consecration of the Rt. Rev. Dr. Seabury to the episcopal office is valid.' The convention adjourned on August 6, 1789, to reassemble in Christ Church on September 29. The Rt. Rev. Samuel Seabury attended, conferred with the convention, and presented his letters of consecration which were read and recorded. As a result, on October 3, 1789, it was announced that there were now a sufficient number of bishops present to enable the two houses to meet separately. The bishops then withdrew from the House of Clerical and Lay Deputies and met separately as the House of Bishops, whereupon the House of Clerical and Lay Deputies elected a chairman and proceeded to the work of ecclesiastical unification and liturgical revision.

Article 8 of the ecclesiastical constitution as adopted read:

A book of common prayer, administration of the sacraments, and other rites and ceremonies of the church,

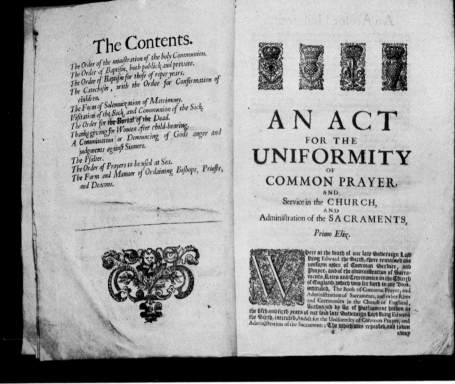

The Contents.

The Order of the ministration of the holy Communion.
The Order of Baptism, both publick and private.
The Order of Baptism for those of riper years.
The Catechism, with the Order for Confirmation of children.
The Form of Solemnization of Matrimony.
Visitation of the Sick, and Communion of the Sick.
The Order for the Burial of the Dead.
Thanksgiving for Women after child-bearing.
A Commination or Denouncing of Gods anger and judgements against Sinners.
The Psalter.
The Order of Prayers to be used at Sea.
The Form and Manner of Ordaining Bishops, Priests, and Deacons.

AN ACT
FOR THE
UNIFORMITY
OF
COMMON PRAYER,
AND
Service in the CHURCH,
AND
Administration of the SACRAMENTS,

Primo Eliz.

Here at the death of our late Soveraign Lord King Edward the Sixth, there remained one uniform order of Common Service, and Prayer, and of the administration of Sacraments, Rites and Ceremonies in the Church of England, which was set forth in one Book, intituled, The Book of Common Prayer, and Administration of Sacraments, and other Rites and Ceremonies in the Church of England, Authorised by Act of Parliament holden in the fifth and sixth years of our said late Soveraign Lord King Edward the Sixth, intituled, An Act for the Uniformity of Common Prayer, and Administration of the Sacraments: The which was repealed and taken away

Photo by T. Horydczak, Washington

THE ORIGINAL 1662 BOOK OF COMMON PRAYER, published in London by His Majesty's Printers. This book, owned by Washington Cathedral Library, is shown open to An Act for the Uniformity of Common Prayer, enacted in the reign of Queen Elizabeth. The design of the title page was executed by D. Loggan, Sculp. The pages measure 7 by 11½ inches. The Book was set forth as a result of the Savoy Conference held by the presbyterian and the episcopal clergy of the Church of England. The presbyterian group presented a revised Book which, though rejected, influenced the final form. The result of the Savoy Conference and the restoration of the Church of England was actually a revision of the 1636 Black Letter Book, but the Durham Prayer Book of John Cosin also profoundly influenced the ultimate content. In order that there should be standard copies available for examination in cases of dispute, and that no unauthorized alterations might be made in public worship, the great Seal of England was attached to certain copies, and these standard volumes were placed in the cathedrals, in the courts of Westminster, and in the Tower of London. In his *Annotated Book of Common Prayer*, the Rev. John Henry Blunt pictures a sealed copy of the 1662 Book of Common Prayer, open to Trinity Sunday XIV. The Washington Cathedral copy agrees with this and, if not a Sealed Book, is evidently of the same edition.

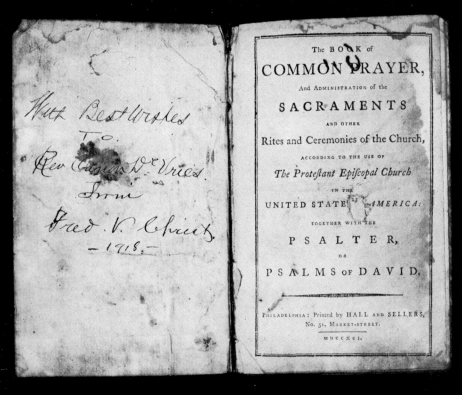

THE 1790 PRE-STANDARD EDITION OF THE BOOK OF COMMON PRAYER, TITLE PAGE OF THE 1791 IMPRESSION. This Book was set forth by the General Convention of 1789, held in Christ Church, Philadelphia. Published by Hall and Sellers of Philadelphia, the book is small, the pages measuring 3½ by 5¾ inches. The Book contains the ratification found in all Books of Common Prayer of the Protestant Episcopal Church but lacks any statement to the effect that the 1791 publication is a standard edition or that it conforms to an official text. This 1791 impression of the 1790 Pre-standard Edition lacks the Articles of Religion and the Ordinal; it contains the Metrical Psalter as well as twenty-seven hymns. The phrase 'which we now offer unto thee' in the Oblation of the communion service is printed in small capitals. The edition contains a service, Forms of Prayer to be Used at Sea, which was not to supplant the regular services of the Book. It also contains a Form of Prayer for the Visitation of Prisoners, derived from the 1711 Irish Book of Common Prayer. The text was compiled by the 1789 General Convention from the Proposed Book of 1785, the English Book of 1662, the Irish Book of 1711, and the communion service of Bishop Samuel Seabury. The latter may be traced to the first Book of 1549 through the Book of 1637, which in turn was compiled by Scottish bishops in the time of Archbishop Laud and was rejected by the Church of Scotland. Washington Cathedral Library owns the book shown here.

articles of religion, and a form and manner of making, ordaining, and consecrating, Bishops, Priests, Deacons, when established by this or a future General Convention, shall be used in the Protestant Episcopal Church in those states which shall have adopted this constitution.[4]

October 3, 1789, the convention began work on the production of the Book of Common Prayer. No one alluded to the Proposed Book. The House of Bishops acted on the assumption that the 1662 Book of Common Prayer of the Church of England was being revised to meet national needs; the House of Clerical and Lay Deputies acted on the assumptions that no book existed and that they were creating one. Five committees on Book of Common Prayer creation were chosen in the House of Clerical and Lay Deputies and charged with the creation of particular portions of it. The committee to prepare a Calendar, Tables of Lessons, and Collects, Epistles, and Gospels consisted of the Rev. Drs. Parker and Moore, the Rev. Messrs. Bend and Jarvis, and Dr. Clarkson. The committee to prepare 'a morning and evening service for the use of the church' consisted of the Rev. Drs. Robert Smith and Blackwell, the Rev. Mr. Hubbard, and Messrs. Rumsey and Andrews. To prepare a Litany and Occasional Prayers and Thanksgivings, the Rev. Dr. Beach, the Rev. Messrs. Bracken and Bisset, and Messrs. Hopkinson and Goldsborough were selected. The committee on an Order for the Administration of the Holy Communion consisted of the Rev. Messrs. Pilmore, Ogden, and Frazer, Col. Ogden, and Mr. Sykes. Appointed to prepare the Psalter were Messrs. Andrews and Hopkinson, and the Rev. Drs. Moore, Parker, and Robert Smith.

The Prayer Book which was adopted by the General

[4] *Ibid.*, Article 8, Ecclesiastical Constitution Adopted 1789, Appendix, p. 328.

Convention of 1789 was in reality the 1662 Book of Common Prayer of the Church of England, revised and enriched in the light of the Proposed Book, the Irish Book of Common Prayer, the Scottish Book of Common Prayer, and the opinions of the bishops and deputies in convention assembled. This revision was ordered in use 'from the first day of October 1790.' [5] Final work on the Book having been completed Friday, October 16, 1789, the lower house appointed a committee (the Rev. Drs. William Smith, Magaw, and Blackwell, and Messrs. Hopkinson and Cose) to superintend the printing and requested the House of Bishops to appoint a similar committee. The Rt. Rev. William White was appointed to represent the House of Bishops. The Book was printed by Hall and Sellers of Philadelphia in 1790. This Pre-standard Edition of the Book of Common Prayer went through two printings. Though the editions of 1790, 1791, and 1792 were not standard editions or standard books, they were followed by six standard editions, beginning with that of 1793, which was printed by Hugh Gaine 'By Order of the General Convention.' It was the first edition to carry that designation. The Standard Editions of 1793, 1822, 1832, 1838, 1845, and 1871 were followed by the first Standard Book of 1892, and the second Standard Book of 1928.

Errors having crept into the Book of Common Prayer, either by accident or design, the General Convention of 1792 created a joint committee 'to examine the printed Book by the original acts of the 1789 Convention and to prepare a mode for authenticating the book by some certain standard, and of publishing future editions of the same in the churches in the different states.' The members of the joint committee from the House of Clerical and Lay Deputies were the Rev. Drs. Magaw and Moore, the Rev. Mr.

---

[5] *Book of Common Prayer of the Protestant Episcopal Church*, Ratification.

Jarvis, Col. Ogden, John De Hart, Esq., and Dr. Hindman. The bishops were Seabury and White. During the convention a resolution was introduced calling for the establishment of a committee with power to obtain a copyright on behalf of the General Convention, to grant the right to publish the Book, and to correct errors according to some standard book. All of this indicates that neither a standard book nor a standard edition existed.

The 1801 General Convention, which met in Trenton, New Jersey, enacted legislation seeking to standardize the text of the Book of Common Prayer and to regulate its publication so that the editions published should agree with the text set forth by the Church in General Convention. Canon III as adopted by this Convention reads:

The Bishop of this Church, in any state or, where there is no Bishop, the standing committee are authorized to appoint, from time to time, some suitable person or persons to compare and correct all new editions of the common prayer book, book of offices, &c. by some standard book; and a certificate of their having been so compared and corrected shall be published with said books. And in case any edition shall be published without such correction it shall be the duty of the Bishop, or, where there is no Bishop, of the standing committee to give public notice that such edition is not authorized by the Church. The Bishop of this Church in Pennsylvania, is hereby authorized to set forth an edition of the articles of religion, which, when published shall be the standard copy. The octavo edition of the common prayer book, published in New York in 1793, by Hugh Gaine, and the quarto edition of the book of offices, &c. of the same year, published in the same place, are hereby established as the standard books, with the exception of errors evidently typographical; the correction of which errors is confided to such person or persons as the Bishop or standing committee may appoint for superintending such publication.[6]

The General Convention of 1808 added an amendment to the article on the Prayer Book. It read: 'No alteration or addition shall be made in the Book of Common Prayer, or other offices in the Church, unless the same shall be proposed in one general convention and by a resolve thereof made known to the convention of every diocese or state, and adopted at the subsequent general convention.'[7] Prior to this, a General Convention could alter the Book of Common Prayer during one session.

The text of the Book of Common Prayer remained almost unchanged from the first Standard Edition of 1793 until the first Standard Book of 1892. In the General Convention of 1892 the method of authentication was revised. Previously the Book had been considered authentic if it carried a statement of approbation by the bishop or, if there were no bishop, by the standing committee of the diocese in which the edition was set forth. But the General Convention of 1892 adopted the following canon:

No copy or edition of the Book of Common Prayer shall be made, printed, published, or used as of authority in this Church, unless it contain the authorization of the custodian of the Standard Book of Common Prayer, certifying that he or some person appointed by him has compared the said copy or edition with the said Standard or a certified copy thereof, and that it conforms thereto.[8]

[6] *Ibid.*, *Convention of 1801*, Canon III, p. 208.

[7] *Ibid.*, *Convention of 1808*, Resolution VI, Concerning Article 8, p. 253.

[8] *Digest of the Canons of the Protestant Episcopal Church*, printed for the Convention (Boston: Mudge & Son, 1899), Canon 22, Section 5, pp. 84-85.

In conformity with this canon, and on the completion of the work of revision in 1892, a Standard Book of Common Prayer was published and placed in the keeping of the Custodian of the Standard Book, the Rev. Samuel Hart, D.D. That Book, together with the 1928 or second Standard Book of Common Prayer, is now in the custody of the Very Reverend John Wallace Suter, D.D., the present Custodian.

The three most important American Books of Common Prayer are those of 1789, 1892, and 1928. The 1789 Book grew out of not only the 1662 Book of Common Prayer of the Church of England but also the Scottish liturgy through the Office for Holy Communion prepared by Bishop Seabury for the Church in Connecticut. The Seabury Communion Office, which moulded the liturgical shape of our communion service, was derived from the Scottish Book of 1764 and earlier liturgies. Our Order for the Administration of the Holy Communion has been enriched by the insertion of the Prayer of Consecration taken from the Scottish Book. In the 1549 service of Holy Communion the Prayer of Consecration is joined to the Prayer for the Whole State of Christ's Church. In this consecration prayer a one-sentence invocation of the Holy Spirit to sanctify the elements of bread and wine that they may be, to the recipients, the body and blood of Christ, precedes the recitation of the words of institution. This is followed by a rubric forbidding elevation of the consecrated elements. Then follows a prayer (called in our Book the Oblation) slightly different from ours, to which is added part of what we know as the Invocation, within which is an invocation not of the Holy Spirit but of the Angels:

Yet we beseech thee to accept this our bounden duty and service, and command these our prayers and supplications, by the ministry of thy holy Angels, to be brought up into thy holy Tabernacle before the sight of thy divine majesty: not weighing our merits but pardoning our offences . . .

The 1662 Consecration Prayer begins as does ours save for the opening words, 'All glory be to thee.' After asserting the completeness of the sacrifice which Our Lord made on the Cross, there follows:

Hear us, O Merciful Father we most humbly beseech thee and grant that we receiving these thy creatures of bread and wine according to thy Son our Saviour Christ's holy institution in remembrance of his death and passion may be partakers of His most blessed body and blood.

Then follows the recital of the Acts of Institution. There is no Invocation of the Holy Spirit in the Consecration Prayers in this rite.

The 1637 Book prepared by bishops of Scotland under the supervision of Archbishop William Laud agrees with the 1549 Book in inserting a one-sentence invocation into the Prayer of Consecration. The Oblation in this Book speaks not of offering the 'holy gifts' but of making with the 'holy gifts' the memorial which Our Lord has 'willed us to make in remembrance of his blessed passion.' The prayer then includes some of what in our Book is called the Invocation. In this, as in the 1549 Book, the only invocation to the Holy Spirit in the canon comes before the recitation of our Lord's words of Institution. These three rites lack the clarity and the liturgical orderliness of the communion as found in our American Book.

Bishop Seabury was consecrated on the Twenty-third Sunday after Trinity, November 14, 1784. The next day he agreed to do all in his power to have the American Church adopt the Scottish Liturgy used for the celebration of the communion at his consecration. October 14, as a result of Seabury's insistence and their recognition of its liturgical excellence, the 1789 General Convention adopted the Scottish Prayer of Institution, Oblation and Invocation. These portions of the Scottish rite, set forth by Bishop Seabury in the Order of Communion for his diocese, were placed in our Book of 1789 with a slight alteration of pronouns and with a change in the wording of the Invocation of the Holy Spirit on the elements; 'that they may become the body and blood of thy most dearly beloved Son,' became 'that we, receiving them according to thy Son our Saviour Jesus Christ's holy Institution, in remembrance of his Death and Passion, may be partakers of his most blessed Body and Blood.' So changed, the Scottish prayers of Consecration, Oblation, and Invocation have appeared in all subsequent editions of the American Book of Common Prayer. They are traceable to the Scottish Books of 1755 and of 1744, Deacon's Liturgy of 1734, and the Non-Juror's Book of 1718. General Convention adopted this part of Seabury's service because the delegates saw in it all the excellences of the English Rite of 1662 and, in addition, a more complete and more ancient Canon of Consecration.

The Proposed Book of 1786, although ignored in 1789 by both the House of Bishops and the House of Clerical and Lay Deputies, contributed greatly to the structure of the first American Prayer Book. From that Proposed Book the compilers of the Book of 1789 took the two sentences at the beginning of Morning and Evening Prayer ('The Lord is in His Holy Temple . . .' and 'From the Rising of the sun even unto the going down of the same . . .'); the General Confession in Morning and Evening Prayer; and the innovation, not in the 1662 Book, of using the Gloria in Excelsis after the Psalms in Morning Prayer. The Book of 1789 followed the Proposed Book also in omit-

ting the Athanasian Creed and altering the Te Deum and
the marriage service. To the framers of the Proposed
Book we owe the phrase in the Te Deum, 'thou didst
humble thyself to be born of a virgin,' in place of 'thou
didst not abhor the Virgin's womb'; and the exclusion
from the marriage service of the words, 'with my body
I thee worship.' The Proposed Book adopted the Office for
the Visitation of Prisoners from the Irish Book of 1711,
and the compilers of 1789 followed their example. This
was kept in all editions until 1928. The wisdom of the
compilers of the Proposed Book is probably manifested by
their making optional in those days the use of the sign
of the cross in baptism and by their allowing parents to
serve as sponsors for their children. These permissions
remained until the Book of 1928, when the sign of the
cross was made mandatory. The Proposed Book gave to
the Book of 1789 the alterations of the 1662 sacramental
portion of the Catechism. This reads not, 'the body and
blood of Christ which are *verilly and indeed* taken and
received by the faithful in the Lord's supper' but *spiritually*
received. The Proposed Book of 1786 contained a Form
of Prayer and Thanksgiving to Almighty God for the
Inestimable Blessings of Religious and Civil Liberty, to
be used yearly on the Fourth Day of July, unless it hap-
pens to fall on Sunday, and then to be used on the day
following. This the compilers of the Book of 1789 unfor-
tunately failed to incorporate in the first American Book,
because of the position taken by Bishop William White.
However, a token of it appears in the Collect, Epistle,
Gospel, and Lessons for Independence Day, added in 1928.

The 1662 Book of Common Prayer, which formed the
groundwork of the 1789 Book, was in some places altered
to conform to changed political conditions. The Prayer
for the King was transformed into a Prayer for the President of the United States and all others in authority, the

Prayer for the High Court of Parliament was changed into one for the Congress of the United States of America, and the Commination Service contributed to the Penitential Office for Ash Wednesday.

An innovation of rich spiritual significance in 1789 was the addition of a section called Forms of Prayer to be Used in Families. This was a small assortment of morning and evening prayers for use in Church families. The prayers were written by the Rt. Rev. Edmund Gibson, Bishop of London, a cleric termed by the Rev. John Wesley 'a great man eminent for his learning.' The prayers have remained in all subsequent editions.

The 1892 Standard Book was the fruit of twelve years of struggle for liturgical revision and enrichment. To the Rev. William Reed Huntington, more than anyone else, is due the praise of the Church for having forced her out of liturgical inertia and impelled her to begin the work of relating her worship more explicitly to the needs of contemporary man. The 1892 Standard Book of Common Prayer differed from the Pre-standard Edition of 1789 and the Standard Editions of 1793-1871 in that five new sentences of Holy Scripture were added to the offertory section of the service of Holy Communion [9] and fifteen new sentences to the introductory portions of Morning Prayer; [10] the Magnificat and the Nunc Dimittis were added to Evening Prayer in their traditional positions; the patriotic spirit of the Protestant Episcopal Church was expressed by the insertion of a prayer for the President which is still in use in Evening Prayer; the Litany was enriched by the addition of a petition, 'That it may please thee to send forth laborers into thy harvest'; the number of occasional prayers was increased by the addition of the

[9] William McGarvey, *Liturgiae Americanae* (Philadelphia: Sunshine Publishing Co., 1895), pp. 94-98.
[10] *Ibid.*, pp. 224-226.

present Prayer for Unity which was derived from the 1662 Accession Service, the Prayer for Missions which was written by Bishop B. P. Cotton of Calcutta in 1861 and revised in 1928 to purge it of its extreme Calvinism, and the Prayer for Fruitful Seasons which was compiled by Bishop Whitehead of Pittsburgh. New Collects, Epistles, and Gospels were inserted for the first communion on Christmas and on Easter Day, and a Collect, Epistle, and Gospel were provided for the Feast of the Transfiguration, which was set for August 6. The growing custom of non-communicating high masses was discouraged by the adoption of a communion rubric requiring that 'sufficient opportunity shall be given to those present to communicate.' The marriage service was altered by the insertion of a statement that marriage is 'an honorable estate instituted of God in the time of man's innocency'—an assertion deleted in 1928. The Nicene Creed was ordered used in the service of Ordination of Presbyters and in the service for the Consecration of Bishops. Three prayers were added to the Burial Office, giving the officiating clergyman greater opportunity to be of help to bereaved people. Permission to shorten the Office of Communion for the Sick was a proper move, in line with the growing understanding of the psychological factors involved. A move to provide wider choice of Lessons and Psalms was made by the adoption of Tables for the Selection of Psalms, and Tables of Proper Psalms for Fast and Feast Days. Here the 1892 revision began a liturgical movement which found fuller fruition in 1928.

The Standard Book of Common Prayer, as revised and enriched by the 1892 General Convention, which met in Baltimore, was placed in the care of the Rev. Samuel Hart, D.D., as Custodian. Dr. Hart was then rector of Trinity Church, Hartford, Connecticut. He was followed, as Custodian of the Standard Book, by the Rev. Lucien M.

Robinson, who in turn was succeeded in 1932 by the Rev. John Wallace Suter, D.D. On his death he was succeeded by his son, the Rev. John Wallace Suter, D.D., now Dean of Washington Cathedral.

Dr. William Reed Huntington and all others interested in the liturgical revision of the Book of Common Prayer felt the work accomplished in 1892 was incomplete, and therefore in 1913 a joint committee was appointed to report on the need for such revision and enrichment as would adapt the Prayer Book to present conditions. Fifteen years of liturgical study, the experience of World War I, an increased awareness of man's responsibility for his fellow men, the impelling need to relate scientific truth to the truths of the Gospel, the increased sensitivity to the needs of anxious, bewildered, and distraught people—all combined to impel the commission to undertake alterations which have proved of value to the moral and devotional life of the Church.

The 1928 revision brought new flexibility and new material. A wide range of permissive Scripture readings and use of the Psalms make possible a more enlightening and inspiring worship. The various permissives for shortening the services increase the sustained interest of the worshipper. If these are wisely used by the officiant, they may contribute to greater devotion and richer spiritual growth; if they are unwisely used they contribute to spiritual impoverishment. The elimination of twelve of the Offertory Sentences in Holy Communion which stressed personal responsibility for responding to individual needs through Christian acts of charity, was of questionable wisdom. The Book was greatly enriched by the insertion of Proper Prefaces for the feasts of the Epiphany, the Purification, the Annunciation, the Transfiguration, and All Saints' Day. The service of Holy Communion was changed to permit the Ten Commandments to be read in a shortened form and to be omitted on all but one Sunday in the month. This permission runs the danger of lessening the worshipper's consciousness of the moral imperatives of the Gospel. A rubric was inserted allowing a gradual hymn to be sung between the Epistle and the Gospel. The scope of the Prayer for the Whole State of Christ's Church Militant was expanded to include the blessed dead—by addition of the words 'And we also bless thy holy Name for all thy servants departed this life in thy faith and fear; beseeching thee to grant them continual growth in thy love and service,' etc. The word 'Militant' was deleted from the title to indicate the blessed dead were included in the prayer. Other prayers for the departed were incorporated in the Burial Office and in Family Prayers, thus showing the Church's appreciation of the oneness of this life with that which is beyond. The long exhortation, to be said after the Prayer for Christ's Church Militant and required to be read one Sunday in each month, was made optional on all days save the First Sunday in Advent, the First Sunday in Lent, and Trinity Sunday. The Prayer of Humble Access was moved from before the Consecration to immediately after the Lord's Prayer, where both are to be said before the reception of communion.

The three services of Baptism were combined, with rubrical directives adapting the service to the baptism of either infants or adults. A revision in the direction of humility and mercy, as well as truth, was the deletion from the Baptismal Office of the statement that the unbaptized child is 'conceived and born in sin,' as was the deletion from the Penitential Office of the phrase 'vile earth,' which the 1892 Book placed upon the Christian's lips and which savors of the doctrine of the total depravity of mankind. In the interest of Christian charity the rubrical prohibition against using the Burial Office for a person who has committed suicide was withdrawn, and a gift of inestimable value was given the Church in the new Office for the Burial of a Child.

The Catechism, logically divisible into two parts, was made into two Offices of Instruction. These Offices have been of value in church schools and are used frequently with the services of Morning and Evening Prayer, to the interest and advantage of many churchmen.

A committee consisting of Bishops William Cabell Brown, A. C. A. Hall, and William F. Faber, the Rev. Messrs. Lucien M. Robinson, John W. Suter, Hughell E. W. Fosbroke, and E. De S. Juny, and Messrs. George Zabriskie and C. S. Baldwin was appointed to study the Psalter and bring before General Convention such revision as was deemed requisite in the interest of textual accuracy. The convention in a few instances declined the suggestions of the committee but for the most part adopted its recommendations.

Certain changes were made by the 1928 Convention in the marriage service. The promises exacted of both the man and the woman were made identical; the word obey, and the clause 'with all my worldly goods I thee endow' were removed; and a prayer for the blessing of the ring was inserted. The reference to the faithfulness of Isaac and Rebecca was eliminated and two new prayers were added, one for the gift of children and the other for the establishment of a home of blessing and of peace.

Over one hundred prayers were added to the Book. They cover many fields of human endeavor and aspiration. Christian concern for good government is emphasized by the new Prayer for the President and by the Prayer for a Legislature. Christian education is brought before God in the Prayer for Religious Education (p. 42), and the Prayer for Children (p. 43). The needs of the Church Catholic are recognized in Archbishop William Laud's great Prayer for the Church (p. 37). Participation in the missionary work of the Church is assured those who will offer the Prayers for Missions (p. 38). The Prayer For Our Country (p. 36), written by the Rev. George Lyman Locke, rector of St. Michael's Church, Bristol, Rhode Island, grants good citizens a Christian means of dedicating the land they love to the God who made it.

The additional prayers of 1928 have become of inestimable help to those who in this modern age have sought guidance in living, increase of faith, and clarity of vision. There is a richness in the Book of Common Prayer—a richness which has been made possible because the Book has grown during four hundred years out of the experiences and the needs of the many as well as the spiritual insights of the few.

CHAPTER V

THE PRAYER BOOK TODAY

WE HAVE followed the development of the American Prayer Book, and have seen how it came to be what it is. Let us now look at it *as* it is. What does it say? What does it mean? How is it intended to be used?

The contents of the Book may profitably be regarded from several points of view. One may see it with the eyes of the officiating clergyman who asks, How does it direct me to lead my congregation in acts of public worship? Or one may examine its six hundred pages as devotional literature and analyze the materials under such headings as purpose, liturgical movement, and style. Again, a student may find between its covers a system of regulations governing not only ceremonial but also daily life; a guide for the meeting of crises, personal and social; and a pattern of behavior while worshipping in the assembly. Or one may use the Book to chart his course through an annual schedule of private Bible reading. All such avenues of study invite our attention; each is rewarding in its own way. But the present chapter speaks to the layman who has made up his mind to join the branch of the Christian Church which has adopted this Book of Common Prayer, and who asks, What does the Prayer Book provide for me? Into what experiences shall I enter because my Church has this Book?

Your Church believes that the Bible is the Word of

God, and that it has something to say to your soul. There is not a day in your life when the Prayer Book does not expect you to read and ponder a passage of Scripture (pp. vii-xlv).

Your Church believes in the drama of the seasons, and in your inherent responsiveness to such a drama, knowing you to be susceptible to suggestion, to vivid imagery, to the fascination of an unfolding plot. Matching the drama of nature, which is controlled by the journey of the earth around the sun, the Church has built up a dramatic seasonal story of its own in which Christ is the center, and we, each of us an immortal soul, lead lives that revolve around Him and His life, our own days being full of waywardness and stumbling, but there being always the (literally) redeeming feature that our spirits have the strong tendency to be held in God's orbit when we yield our wills to Him (pp. xlvi-lvii).

You will meet with your fellow worshippers to offer up to the Eternal the praise and supplication of divine service in Morning or Evening Prayer. This is a corporate act wherein the fellowship of believers, the blessed company, forgetting self for a brief hour and thinking only of God, pours out its love and adoration to Him as it listens with reverence to His Word and seeks a renewal of His gifts. 'O send out thy light and thy truth, that they may lead me. . . Thus saith the high and lofty One that inhabiteth eternity . . . the true worshippers shall worship the Father in spirit and in truth' (p. 3). You will meet with your fellow townspeople 'to render thanks for the great benefits received at God's hands, to set forth his most worthy praise, to hear his most holy Word' (p. 6).

You will confess your sinfulness: orally, in concert with the sinful community of which you are a part; you will ask forgiveness; you will receive forgiveness; you will recite the Lord's Prayer, partly as an asking, but partly

Photo by T. Horydczak, Washington

THE 1892 STANDARD BOOK OF COMMON PRAYER. This is the first Standard Book of Common Prayer of the Protestant Episcopal Church in the United States of America. The volume is executed on vellum with red rulings, bound in violet crushed levant. The pages measure 9½ by 14 inches. The book has three silver clasps and four silver bosses bearing the symbols of the four Evangelists. The lettering reads: 'This Volume is the Standard Book of Common Prayer of the Protestant Episcopal Church in the United States of America, set forth by the General Convention holden in Baltimore in the year of our Lord MDCCCXCII.' This historical book is in Washington Cathedral in the keeping of the Very Reverend John Wallace Suter, D.D., Custodian of the Standard Book of Common Prayer.

THE 1928 STANDARD BOOK OF COMMON PRAYER. It is certified by Charles
L. Pardee, secretary, House of Bishops; Ze Barney Phillips, president,
House of Deputies; and Carroll M. Davis, secretary, House of Deputies;
and contains a letter from John G. Murray, Presiding Bishop, express-
ing approval of the final proofs. The pages measure 9 by 11½ inches.
October 20, 1928, the House of Bishops stated: 'That the copy of the
Standard Prayer Book of 1892, as presented, revised by the action of
General Conventions from 1913 to 1928 . . . is adopted as the text of
the Standard Book of Common Prayer.' This book is in Washington
Cathedral in the keeping of the Very Reverend John Wallace Suter,
D.D., Custodian of the Standard Book of Common Prayer. It is the
standard text in use in America today.

also to remind yourself of the standard set for your life by Him whom you acknowledge to be your life's Master (pp. 6, 7).

The reading of the Scripture is a sacramental act—outward, visible, audible; but full of grace and truth, which are inward, invisible, and direct from God. When the minister goes to the lectern to read the Bible to you, he treads with reverent foot, for here, as actually as at that other symbol of the Presence, the altar, he 'handles things unseen'; here, as there, he mediates to you God Himself, who is Spirit (pp. 9 and 14).

You will declare your Christian faith and allegiance: your ultimate trust in God the Father Almighty . . . in Christ the Lord . . . in the Holy Ghost, the Catholic Church, the Communion of Saints, the Life everlasting (p. 15).

You will say or sing praises. You will let your imagination be stirred by the great words of the liturgy, feeling your oneness with millions of worshippers through the centuries, with other millions over the earth today, and still others yet unborn. You will meditate; you will make a resolution; you will be startled by a new insight. The service ends; you pause a moment in silence, then leave to go back into the ordinary world of bread-winning, social engagements, battles with sickness, temptation, fatigue, bewilderment; but you take back with you a finer vision, refreshment, a better sense of direction, and a deeper awareness of the immortal framework in which your life is set.

Some morning you will rise early and set off to church with a special feeling in your heart, a feeling that you are going to meet not only your fellow Christians, not only your minister, not only the everliving God of all the ages, but God as particularly revealed and self-given in and through the Sacrament of the Body and Blood of

Christ, who 'did vouchsafe to yield up his soul by death upon the Cross for your salvation,' and who is your 'spiritual food and sustenance in that holy Sacrament' (pp 89, 87). This service has a long and self-examining preparation, which challenges you by the Ten Commandments, and by our Lord's summary of them when He bids you love your God and your neighbor. It reminds you that God's world is a world of law (pp. 68, 69). You are given an opportunity to measure your spiritual development against the standard set by readings from the Bible, and by the Creed (pp. 70, 71). It confronts you with the searching question of your stewardship of worldly goods: are you generous? are you honest in your financial dealings? do you treat wealth as a trust from God, from whom all things come? (pp. 72, 73). It bids you pray for the whole of Christ's Church—not just your parish, or your branch of Anglicanism, or even Anglicanism as a whole, but the entire Church of Christ as such: all who confess His holy Name, all Christian rulers, all ministers, all God's people, all who are in trouble, all who have died in faith (pp. 74, 75). This is a tremendous coverage. How many of us really and honestly care what becomes of such an illimitable concourse of people—of all colors, all languages, and vastly differing types of religion? For the Christian Church, potentially a fellowship, actually is split into groups that frequently differ. Yet, for all these you must pray if you would approach the Lord's Table to receive the Bread of Heaven.

You confess your sins, and in somewhat extreme language, for you see them as committed 'against his Divine Majesty.' 'The burden of them is intolerable.' This burden is then miraculously removed; from it God delivers you, and saves your soul alive: not for any merit of yours, but by reason of the redeeming power of the Son whom God sent into the world to rescue you from the power of sin (pp. 75, 76).

Relieved of your spiritual burden, you 'lift up your heart unto the Lord,' joining with priest and people in what is one of the Prayer Book's most sublime expressions of praise:

> Therefore with Angels and Archangels, and with all the company of heaven, we laud and magnify thy glorious Name; evermore praising thee, and saying,
>
> Holy, Holy, Holy, Lord God of hosts, Heaven and earth are full of thy glory: Glory be to thee, O Lord Most High. *Amen.*[1]

You are now ready to listen with rapt attention while the priest reverently reads the wonderful Prayer of Consecration (pp. 80, 81). In the first three paragraphs the congregation and priest are jointly involved in the act of solemnly consecrating—that is, rendering sacred and holy, so that they become charged with divine efficacy—the bread and wine which are to be the efficient signs and symbols of Christ's Presence, the means by which that Presence, which is spiritual, is conveyed to the hearts and consciences of those who receive in faith what Jesus Himself told them to receive. This is a holy and mysterious transaction, differently interpreted by different people even within the same ecclesiastical fellowship. And it is right that these differences should obtain, for they are the guarantee of sincerity, without which the great communion would be a sham.

Leaving your pew and going to the altar rail, you kneel, and there, side by side with other members of Christ's Church, as a symbol of the universality of this 'blessed company' whose table extends around the earth, you 'feed on him in your heart by faith, with thanksgiving' (p. 82).

---

[1] *Book of Common Prayer,* p. 77.

Afterwards, before the service ends, you say one of the most important 'Amens' that you ever say, for it is your assent to the petition that you may continue in the holy fellowship of the mystical body of Christ, and do all such good works as God has prepared for you (p. 83). In other words, this great service, so filled with drama and poetry and mystery, so explicitly linked with heaven, brings you down to earth and sends you out into the busy world with a commitment to live better.

If you marry, the new relationship will be entered into reverently, soberly, in the fear of God and before his holy altar, in the presence of witnesses, and in a ceremony presided over by a priest of the Church, though not he but you and your bride will be the 'officiants.' The vows you take at that time, searching and solemn in their own right, become even more so by being made in the Name and Presence of the Almighty (pp. 300-304). The Prayer Book gives you the choice of having this service just by itself, or in connection with a special celebration of the Holy Communion, whose Collect prays that you and your wife, seeking first God's kingdom and His righteousness, may obtain the manifold blessings of His grace (p. 267).

If a child is born to you, the Prayer Book provides a service in which he is 'received into Christ's holy Church,' and by the Holy Spirit 'born again'—born, that is, into the spiritual family we call the Church of Christ (pp. 273-281). When he is old enough to understand, he will be taught in terms of the Prayer Book Offices of Instruction, learning about Baptism, the Creed, the Ten Commandments, the Lord's Prayer, the nature of the Church (including his duties and privileges as a member), and the sacraments (pp. 283-295). Later, on a day when the bishop of your diocese visits your parish, your child will receive the Laying on of Hands, or Confirmation, wherein, after renewing the promises and vows of his Baptism, and declaring his loyalty and devotion to Christ as his Master, he will receive the strengthening gifts of that same Holy Spirit whose presence in his life was assured and bestowed at his Baptism (pp. 296-299). Furthermore, the Prayer Book furnishes you and your wife and children with prayers, and suggested forms, for use at home when the family gather for daily devotions, either at the breakfast table or at some other place and hour: prayers which take account of the stresses and strains, as well as the joys and satisfactions, of family and community life between Sundays. Assuming you would not sit down to eat an unblessed meal, the Book provides two versions of 'Grace before Meat,' one of them asking God to make us mindful of the needs of others (the Family Prayer section at the back of the Book).

As very few individuals, and certainly no families, wholly escape illness, the Prayer Book gives many healing thoughts and words to sustain you and your loved ones, whatever trials of this sort you may be called upon to endure. You are directed to notify your minister, 'who, coming into the sick person's presence, shall say, "Peace be to this house, and to all that dwell in it"' (p. 308). These words set the tone of the Church's whole attitude toward sickness. On the one hand, disease and accident bring to mortal man pain, anxiety, bitterness, rebelliousness, turmoil of spirit, resentment, disappointment, and fear. On the other, into this situation involving both the patient and the family, the Church comes with its strong voice of authority, its sense of God's Presence, its reminder of the always available companionship of the living Christ, friend of sinners and of sufferers. 'O Lord, save thy servant who putteth his trust in thee. Send him help from thy holy place, and evermore mightily defend him' (p. 308). 'The Almighty Lord, who is a most strong tower to all those who put their trust in him . . .' (p. 314). The Book provides also a shortened form of the Holy Communion (p. 321), so that the sacrament, with its power to refresh and restore, may be brought to bear upon the situation, which includes the plight of the sufferer, the fatigue and anxiety of the family, the skills and attitudes of doctors and nurses. Not content with these provisions, the Book also encourages the 'ministry of healing through Anointing, or Laying on of Hands.' 'I anoint thee with oil,' says the priest, 'in the Name of the Father, and of the Son, and of the Holy Ghost; beseeching the mercy of our Lord Jesus Christ, that all thy pain and sickness of body being put to flight, the blessing of health may be restored unto thee' (p. 320).

Sickness may be one of the occasions, though by no means the only one, when you will avail yourself of the invitation (p. 88) to go to your rector, 'or to some other Minister of God's Word, and open your grief; that you may receive such godly counsel and advice, as may tend to the quieting of your conscience.' In all these ways, and others like them, the Prayer Book recognizes the close interaction between body and soul. What the Church seeks to promote is summed up in the word 'wholeness,' which for the body means health, and for the soul means soundness, holiness, sanctity, saved-ness. These two areas, so far from being mutually exclusive, are interlocked and interpenetrating. Peace of mind, and the harmony of physical well-being, are two parts of a single condition. A wrong attitude toward God, a wrong mental picture of Him, a faulty attitude toward self, toward an acquaintance, or toward one's sickness—any of these can literally make one sick, or prolong one's illness.

The day will come when a loved one passes through the experience of death. Here again, the Church speaks to you through the Book of Common Prayer. At the time of the death itself, the minister, standing at the bedside, says,

Depart, O Christian soul, out of this world,
In the Name of God the Father Almighty who created
thee.
In the Name of Jesus Christ who redeemed thee.
In the Name of the Holy Ghost who sanctifieth thee.
May thy rest be this day in peace, and thy dwelling-
place in the Paradise of God.[2]

Later, in Church, you hear the unforgettable words, 'I
am the resurrection and the life, saith the Lord: he that
believeth in me, though he were dead, yet shall he live'
(p. 324).

As you listen, there run through your mind words that
you have heard and cherished during the lifetime of the
one who has died, for often through the years you have
knelt beside him, at the altar rail, while the administering
priest has said, both to your loved one and to you, 'Preserve thy body and soul unto everlasting life.' The everlasting life of the body! What does it mean? Surely not the
continuance of this particular clay, even though it bear the
stamp of something more than mortality. What, then?
Presently you catch the intimation of an answer, as the
minister reads the lesson from a letter of St. Paul. 'There
is a natural body, and there is a spiritual body . . . flesh
and blood cannot inherit the kingdom of God . . . this
mortal must put on immortality' (pp. 329, 330). And again,
the Prayer Book provides for the (optional) use of the
Eucharist at the Burial of the Dead, the Collect for the
occasion praying that God, 'who holds all souls in life,'
will grant that we and all who have gone before may enter
into unending joy; or, as worded in the alternate form, may
have entrance into the land of light and joy (p. 268). And
at the graveside, where the facts of bodily death are sternly

[2] *Ibid.*, p. 319.

and starkly faced, the Church's declaration rings out with indestructible assurance,

> I heard a voice from heaven, saying unto me, Write, From henceforth blessed are the dead who die in the Lord: even so saith the Spirit; for they rest from their labours.[3]

These, then, are some of the answers the Prayer Book makes to the inquirer who asks, What does the Book provide for me?

Through the ages, and around the earth, thousands of people have gone to Church with this Book, uttered its prayers, sung praises to God in its words, kept its silences, added the love of their hearts to its adoration and their fervent desires to its petitions, responded to its moods, lived by its disciplines, obeyed its rules, fasted when it bade them fast and feasted when it bade them rejoice, drawn strength from the deep wells of its devotion, gone to rest at night with its powerful phrases making melody in their hearts, and passed to that other rest, at the last, upheld by its assurance of the love of an immortal God whose gift is the gift of eternal life.

The last prayer of the last public service in the Book, that of the Institution of Ministers into Parishes, is remarkably typical. Like many others, it is a compilation; it includes two of the regular Collects for Days, that of the Apostles St. Simon and St. Jude and that of the Fifth Sunday after Trinity, and a quotation from the Te Deum. It has the flowing style of the late eighteenth and early nineteenth century. Adopted in the Diocese of Connecticut in 1799, it was added to the Prayer Book in 1804, and amended four years later by a process very typical of the Book's development. It is offered in behalf of 'all Christians'—a feature entirely characteristic of a Book of Com-

[3] *Ibid.*, p. 333.

mon Prayer which from cover to cover, as also from century to century, reveals itself as a Book for the whole Church. With this prayer, therefore, the present volume may fittingly close.

O Almighty God, who hast built thy Church upon the foundation of the Apostles and Prophets, Jesus Christ himself being the chief cornerstone; Grant that, by the operation of the Holy Ghost, all Christians may be so joined together in unity of spirit, and in the bond of peace, that they may be an holy temple acceptable unto thee. And especially to this Congregation present, give the abundance of thy grace; that with one heart they may desire the prosperity of thy holy Apostolic Church, and with one mouth may profess the faith once delivered to the Saints. Defend them from the sins of heresy and schism; let not the foot of pride come nigh to hurt them, nor the hand of the ungodly to cast them down. And grant that the course of this world may be so peaceably ordered by thy governance, that thy Church may joyfully serve thee in all godly quietness; that so they may walk in the ways of truth and peace, and at last be numbered with thy Saints in glory everlasting; through the merits of the same thy blessed Son Jesus Christ, the gracious Bishop and Shepherd of our souls, who liveth and reigneth with thee and the same Holy Ghost, one God, world without end. *Amen.*[4]

[4] *Ibid.*, p. 565.

SOME NOTED PRAYER BOOKS

IN VARIOUS LIBRARIES AND SEMINARIES

WASHINGTON CATHEDRAL LIBRARY, Washington

The Order for Communion in the Collection of Articles. London: Printed by Richard Grafton. 1547. Third Edition. Anthony Sparrow.
Book of Common Prayer. London: Richard Grafton and Edward Whitchurche. 1549.
Book of Common Prayer. London: King's Printers. 1662.
Book of Common Prayer. Oxford University: John Basket. 1736.
Book of Common Prayer. Philadelphia: Hall and Sellers. 1791.
Book of Common Prayer. New York: Hugh Gaine. 1795.
Book of Common Prayer, Confederate States of America. London: Eyre and Spottiswoode, for J. W. Randolph, Richmond, Va. 1863.

GENERAL THEOLOGICAL SEMINARY LIBRARY, New York

Book of Common Prayer. London: His Majesty's Printers. 1662.
Proposed Book of Common Prayer. Philadelphia: Hall and Sellers. 1786.
Book of Common Prayer. Philadelphia: Hall and Sellers. 1790.

BERKELEY DIVINITY SCHOOL LIBRARY, New Haven, Conn.

Book of Common Prayer. London: James I. 1604.
Proposed Book of Common Prayer. Philadelphia: Hall and Sellers. 1786.
Book of Common Prayer. New York: Hugh Gaine. 1793.
Book of Common Prayer. Boston: 1794.

BEXLEY HALL LIBRARY, Gambier, Ohio

Proposed Book of Common Prayer. Philadelphia: Hall and Sellers. 1786.
First English Reprint of the Proposed Book. London: J. Debrett. 1789.
Book of Common Prayer. London: Robert Barker. 1611.

CHURCH DIVINITY SCHOOL OF THE PACIFIC LIBRARY, Berkeley, Calif.

Book of Common Prayer. Edinburgh: Robert Young. 1637.

PHILADELPHIA DIVINITY SCHOOL LIBRARY, Philadelphia

Proposed Book of Common Prayer. Philadelphia: Hall and Sellers. 1786.
Book of Common Prayer as Abridged by Benjamin Franklin. London: 1773.
Primer. London: Grafton. 1545.
Book of Common Prayer. London: Whytechurche. 1552.
Liturgy from Book of Common Prayer for First Episcopal Church, Boston. 1785.
Book of Common Prayer. London: Bill and Barker. 1662.
First English Reprint of Proposed Book. London: J. Debrett. 1789.
Book of Common Prayer. Philadelphia: Hall and Sellers. 1790.

EPISCOPAL THEOLOGICAL SCHOOL LIBRARY, Cambridge, Mass.

Liturgia, seu Liber Precum Communium. Londini: R. Norton. 1670.
Book of Common Prayer. Philadelphia: Hall and Sellers. 1790.
Book of Common Prayer. New York: Hugh Gaine. 1793.
Book of Common Prayer. Boston: Thomas and Andrews. 1800.

VIRGINIA THEOLOGICAL SEMINARY LIBRARY, Alexandria, Va.

Facsimile Black Letter Book of Common Prayer, 1636. Published for the Royal Commission on Ritual, 1870.
Facsimile of Manuscript Book signed by Convocation. London: Eyre and Spottiswoode, 1661. Facsimile published 1891.
Book of Common Prayer. New York: Thomas Kirk. 1801.
Book of Common Prayer. Boston: Charles Williams. 1811.

MARYLAND DIOCESAN LIBRARY, Baltimore

Proposed Book of Common Prayer. Philadelphia: Hall and Sellers. 1786.
Book of Common Prayer. Philadelphia: Hall and Sellers. 1790.

BIBLIOGRAPHY

SOME SOURCE MATERIAL FOR THE STUDY OF
THE BOOK OF COMMON PRAYER

The Alterations and Additions in the Book of Common Prayer of the Protestant Episcopal Church in the Years 1886, 1889, and 1892. Boston: Printed for the Convention. 1892.

Arnold, J. H. *Anglican Liturgies.* London: Oxford University Press. 1939.

Barry, Alfred. *The Teacher's Prayer Book.* New York: E. & J. B. Young & Co. 1898.

Blomfield, John. *The Eucharistic Canon.* London: S. P. C. K. 1930.

The Book Annexed. Authorized Edition. New York: E. & J. B. Young & Co. 1885.

Bright, William. *Ancient Collects.* Oxford and London: James Parker & Co. 1875.

Chorley, Edward Clowes. *The New American Prayer Book.* New York: The Macmillan Co. 1929.

Collects of the Book of Common Prayer. New York: E. P. Dutton and Co. 1904.

Dearmer, Percy. *The Story of the Prayer Book.* London and New York: Oxford University Press. 1933.

Dix, Dom Gregory. *The Shape of the Liturgy.* Westminster: Dacre Press. 1947.

Doctrine in the Church of England. Report of the Commission on Christian Doctrine appointed by the Archbishops of Canterbury and York in 1922. New York: The Macmillan Co. 1938.

Driver, S. P. *The Parallel Psalter, being the Prayer Book Version of the Psalms.* Second Edition. Oxford: Clarendon Press. 1904.

Frere, W. H. *Some Principles of Liturgical Reform.* London: John Murray. 1911.

Gasquet, F. A., and Bishop, E. *Edward VI and the Book of Common Prayer.* London: John Hodges. 1890.

Gee, Henry, and Hardy, William John. *Documents Illustrative of English Church History.* London: The Macmillan Co. 1921

Harford, George, and Stevenson, Morley. *The Prayer Book Dictionary.* New York: Longmans, Green & Co. 1912.

Hart, Samuel. *The Book of Common Prayer.* Sewanee, Tenn.: University Press. 1913.

Hart, Samuel. *Bishop Seabury's Communion Office.* New York: Thomas Whittaker. 1883.

Huntington, William Reed. *A Short History of the Book of Common Prayer.* New York: Thomas Whittaker. 1893.

Hurlbut, S. A. *Greek Orthodox Liturgy of St. John Chrysostom, Arranged for Use in English.* Washington: St. Alban's Press. 1942.

Hurlbut, S. A. *The Liturgy of the Church of England.* Washington: St. Alban's Press. 1941.

Jones, Bayard Hale. *The American Lectionary.* New York: Morehouse-Gorham Co. 1944.

Journals of General Convention, 1784 to 1814. Philadelphia: John Bioren. 1817.

Ladd, William Palmer. *Prayer Book Interleaves.* London and New York: Oxford University Press, Inc. 1942.

Liturgy in the Parish. Six Alcuin Club Tracts. London: A. R. Mowbray Co.

McGarvey, William. *Liturgiae Americanae.* Philadelphia: Sunshine Publishing Co. 1895.

Morison, Stanley. *English Prayer Books.* London and New York: Oxford University Press. 1943.

Muller, James Arthur. *Who Wrote the New Prayers in the Prayer Book?* Philadelphia: Church Historical Society. 1946.

Parsons, Edward Lambe, and Jones, Bayard Hale. *The American Prayer Book.* New York: Charles Scribner's Sons. 1937.

Pell, Walden, and Dawley, P. M. *The Religion of the Prayer Book.* New York: Morehouse-Gorham Co. 1943.

Pepper, George Wharton. *An Analytical Index to the Book of Common Prayer.* Philadelphia: John C. Winston Co. 1948.

Perry, William Stevens. *The American Episcopal Church.* Boston: J. R. Osgood & Co. 1885.

Proctor and Frere. *A New History of the Book of Common Prayer.* London: The Macmillan Co. 1920.

Pullan, Leighton. *The History of the Book of Common Prayer.* New York: Thomas Whittaker. 1893.

Rattray, Thomas. *The Ancient Liturgy of the Church of Jerusalem.* London: James Bettenham. 1744.

Robinson, H. Wheeler. *The Bible in Its Ancient and English Versions.* London and New York: Oxford University Press. 1940.

Shepherd, Massie Hamilton, Jr. *The Living Liturgy.* London and New York: Oxford University Press. 1946.

The Shorter Prayer Book According to the Use of the Church of England. London and New York: Oxford University Press.

Suter, John Wallace, Jr. *The Book of English Collects.* New York: Harper & Brothers. 1940.

Suter, John Wallace, Sr. *Life and Letters of William Reed Huntington.* London and New York: The Century Co. 1925.

Suter, John Wallace, Sr., and Addison, Charles Morris. *The People's Book of Worship.* New York: The Macmillan Co. 1919.

Wheatley, Charles. *Rational Illustration of the Book of Common Prayer.* London: George Bell & Sons. 1875.

Wright, John. *Early Prayer Books of America.* St. Paul, Minn. (privately printed). 1896.

DATE DUE

GAYLORD			PRINTED IN U.S.A.